How I Earned My
Wrinkles

*Musings on Marriage, Motherhood,
and Menopause*

ANNE BARDSLEY

WINSTON PUBLISHING
AnzWorld.com

WINSTON PUBLISHING

How I Earned My Wrinkles:
Musings on Marriage, Motherhood, and Menopause

Published in the United States by Winston Publishing

ISBN 978-0-9884792-0-3
AnzWorld.com

Contents

Introduction 1

Acknowledgments 3

Anz World 5

A Weighted Matter 7

Confections and Miracles 9

Memory Lane.. 13

Oh, Those Seven Pounds 16

My Easter Flowers 18

Puppy Training 21

Artsy Jamie 24

Busted 27

Chicken Pox 31

False Alarm 34

Codependency 37

Going Buggy... 39

Gotcha 43

Contrary Attraction 45

Maverick is in the House.. 48

Professionalism 51

Two Old Gals Gone Wild 53

Make Him Notice You All Over Again 59

The Fresh Smell of Spring 63

How I Earned My Wrinkles 65

My Yellow Toes 68

Winston 70

Purple Cow 75

The Hottie Test 78

Disney Trip 81

Mr. Bojangles 84

The Dry Cleaners 88

Toned Up and Tuned In 91

Organization 101 94

Just Call Me Babe 98

Me, Matt, the Cat, and the Watermelon 100

Penguin Petting 103

The Car Wash 107

Sweet Crunches 110

Fluff and Stuff 113

Professional Mourner 116

The Letter of Recommendation 118

Pillow Talk 120

One Hot Mess 122

Senioritis 126

Pretty Pretty 129

The Clothes Bandit 132

Quackers 134

The Note on the Door 136

The Happy Dance 139

The Twelve Days of Hormones 141

The Ugly Baby 143

The Punk on the Beach 145

September Blues 150

Mothers-in-Law 153

Summer Vacation at the Beach 156

My Favorite Gift That I'll Never Receive 159

Introduction

First, I'd like to thank you for reading my book, *How I Earned My Wrinkles: Musings on Marriage, Motherhood, and Menopause.* I hope you smile, laugh, cry, and giggle through the chapters. This adventure has been thirty years in the making (in my mind). Yes, I'm a fan of procrastination!

My inspiration comes from day-to-day life. I grew up in an Irish Catholic family where every day was filled with laughter and storytelling. I'm extra blessed to have Jim and Bette Lawless as my parents. They raised us four girls in a three bedroom, one bath, one phone, and one TV house. My gran also lived with us. We were a very close family, literally. I don't know how my dad ever managed to use the bathroom with that many women under one roof. Can you imagine the flurry of clothes, perfume, and hairballs?

I have a library of journals where I jotted down memories and snippets of conversations I wanted to remember. Actually, I'm not really *that* organized. They aren't so much journals on a shelf as they are a collection of paper napkins, matchbook covers, and restaurant menus stuffed in a drawer with my scribbled notes and tidbits of memories. Sometimes an idea will come to me and I'll write it on the back of a supermarket or bank receipt. I now have a vast collection!

My husband, Scott, loves to balance our checkbook and he'll find those little notes—although he can't always read the numbers of the deposit. Instead, he'll see:

Whose idea was it to buy the little ones musical slippers for Christmas?

If I hear that reindeer song one more time.

Oh no! Justin just covered his belly with toothpaste!

Who told Daddy's mom that she's ugly?

This is my world in little bits and pieces of wonderful (and often humorous) memories.

Acknowledgments

I sincerely, and from the bottom of my heart, thank my sweet husband, Scott. We've been married thirty-five years and our life is blessed. He is my Anam Cara (soul friend) and the love of my life (I really didn't mean all that grumbling I did when he asked me weekly about my stories. I know now he wasn't pestering me).

I must thank my kids, Tom, Mike, Erika, Jamie, and Justin who have been a continuous source of stories. I can honestly say that all five were worth the combined labor pains!

I'd like to thank a very special lady, Jill Haseltine. Jill is my mentor at Toastmasters and a personal coach. She challenged me to make a "Deliberate Decision" (her motto) and I chose to write this book. You can visit her at DeliberateNation.com.

My editor, Anne Younger, is my hero. Her sense of humor and talent with the written word saved me.

Crystal Ponti of Blue Lobster Book Co. is the artistic genius who brought the book to life.

A special thanks to Nancy Frederich at Murmaid Publishing for her sound professional advice.

To many friends who have said over the years, "You should write a book," I did it! I can't remember all of your names, but I definitely remember your faces! Thank you!

And, last but not least, I want to say, "Thank you, God, for my gifts and all of the blessings in my life."

Anz World

Husband, Scott, lost his car keys and wallet for the third time this week.

Daughter, Erika, was late for tennis lessons.

Daughter, Jamie, was practicing backflips in the kitchen.

Son, Tom, was searching in the trash can for his $600 retainer.

Son, Mike, was telling an angry neighbor that it couldn't have been our dog splashing in his expensive koi pond.

The dog was soaking wet and splattering mud all over my new carpet.

Son, Justin, needed his skates sharpened before a hockey game in ten minutes, and we lived twenty minutes away.

The dog threw up koi pond slime on the kitchen floor and the cat's newly arrived kittens were learning to walk ... yes, in the kitchen.

Just then the phone rang.

My mother-in-law was calling to share a few cleaning tips. She also instructed me, "Write this down. It's my lamb chop recipe that Scott loved when he was little. I think your kids need more protein." She fed him lamb chops every blessed day for lunch.

I was about to snap! My mind was spinning. A hot flash was forming like a thundercloud. I seriously needed an escape.

That was the day I invented *Anz World*. It's a place in my mind that is so peaceful and serene some days I never want to leave. This is my special retreat—my refuge from real life—and I have the only key. I can simply take a few deep breaths, close my eyes, and knock on serenity's door. Sometimes I have to lock myself in the bathroom to get some quiet.

Unlike my messy house full of kids, cats, dogs, hamsters, an iguana, and pet snakes, *Anz World* is tidy and clean. It looks like HGTV surprised me and decorated my world. The sky is crystal blue with wispy clouds that resemble angel's wings. There is a gentle island breeze. I even have those sheer white curtains that billow at the open windows.

My hot flashes disappear, as do my wrinkles and cellulite. My face loses years of stress, and I barely recognize myself. I look like a goddess! My short hair is long and luxurious, and my highlights sparkle in the sun. I never need a pedicure. Did I mention that I'm tan and toned? My tan accentuates my newly whitened smile. Seriously, in this place in my mind, I am a goddess.

In my perfect world, Kenny Chesney and Michael Bublé are singing in the background. It's always my favorite songs, and I sing along while I admire my new firm and tan legs. I can't get enough of them!

It's in this place that I can contemplate life. I have time to reminisce and look at the lighter side of my world. I'd had a dream to write this book and, finally, after hiding in *Anz World*, I was able to refocus my energies and bring it to fruition.

I hope you will enjoy the stories. Perhaps you can create your own place of refuge. Call me when you get there. We can meet for tea or a glass of wine. I would love that!

A Weighted Matter

just found out that, for the bulk of my life, I have been exercising the wrong muscles. I'm so depressed.

Years of leg lifts, squats, and miles walked on the treadmill all for naught. I just flipped through the new catalog of *Self-Care Products for Women* and there it was—just in time for my birthday—a vaginal weight set!

The depressing part is that now, in addition to my thighs, buttocks, triceps, and biceps, I have to worry about my hidden parts. I seriously thought they were in great shape. I think I may have even bragged about them at a party after a few glasses of wine. *Why did I ever open that catalog?*

In my family, we never discussed anything below the naval and above the knees. When my dad learned that my aunt was having surgery on her uterus, he asked her if that was close to her Sagittarius.

My mother never mentioned that my sisters and I needed to do Kegels or lift weights with our vaginas. When I was growing up, no one had ever even whispered the actual names of sexual organs at 245 Willow Avenue.

Now there it was in plain print—the word vaginal!

Women didn't have to concern themselves with this stuff in the olden days. Just once, I'd like to open the Sunday paper's fashion section and read, "Scarlett O'Hara hoop dresses are back this season."

I would be such a happy lady! Imagine not having to suck in my stomach, tuck in my derrière, or lift those damned vaginal weights. The hoop dress would hide everything below my waist. Actually, I might need to invest in a corset for above my waist.

The only requirement to look good in a hoop dress is a full bust, and every woman knows that if you just gain a few pounds your bust increases. With a scooped neckline so low, my husband wouldn't even notice if I had a double chin. I doubt he'd even notice I had a face!

So now, in addition to working, cooking, cleaning, carpooling, and my mending (I just slipped that in for Scarlett), I have to tend to more body parts. The ad-men strike again; just one more reminder that I'm not good enough just as I am.

The set only costs $125 and includes a leather carrying case. I envisioned the old, "Don't leave home without it," commercials for American Express. The ad also offers me free shipping if I order an extra set for a friend. I guess they don't realize that I wouldn't have a friend left in the world if I started giving vaginal weight sets as gifts.

The ad assures me that I'll be less embarrassed, more confident, and have more control over my life. They swear that the weights are foolproof.

I think I'd be more embarrassed and less confident if I didn't exercise my self-control and profess that I, too, am foolproof. Who would ever think that bodybuilding a vagina could make such a difference in a woman's life?

As Rhett Butler said, "Frankly, my dear, I don't give a damn!"

ANNE BARDSLEY

Confections
and Miracles

I t was Christmas Eve 1960, and I was seven years old. I'd woken in the dark to pull up my covers closer. The wind was howling, and the tree branches smacked against my window.

"Dear God, please don't let Santa freeze tonight," I prayed. I prayed for everything. Sister Mary Matthew, my second grade teacher, said this was a good thing to do. Just as I finished my prayer a blazing light shot across the sky.

"Was that Santa?" I sprang out of my bed to see. The girls at school were spreading rumors that Santa wasn't real. "Wait until I tell them I saw his sleigh." I smiled and scooted back under the covers.

The next morning, my five-year-old sister, Pat, woke me early. She'd already gone downstairs and peeked under the tree. She was bouncing on my bed screaming at me, "Wake Up! Wake Up!"

As I was rubbing the sleep from my eyes, I noticed white stuff on my bed. It looked like snow. How did that get here? There were footprints on my carpet too. We followed the prints down the stairs, through the dining room, and into the kitchen. That's when we saw it.

"Uh-oh! Somebody is in big trouble," Pat said in a serious tone. There were Snickerdoodle crumbs all over the table and floor. Gran's favorite Irish teacup from Donegal was on the table too. We were never allowed to touch that cup. It was a treasured possession all the way from Ireland.

My little sister's highchair was pulled up to the table. Three phone books were on the seat. What the heck was going on?

Mom and Dad came into the kitchen as we chimed in, "We did not do this! And we didn't touch Gran's tea cup, either." We swore.

Mom looked at us with a doubtful expression when my dad said, "I used it last night."

Oh, he was so brave to admit that!

Pat didn't care. "Let's open presents!" she shouted.

My dad said, "Okay, if you don't want to hear about the elf that was here last night, go right ahead."

I couldn't believe my ears! "An elf? An elf was in my house? Tell me! Tell me!"

Dad told how he was driving home late from work when something moved in the snow. He thought it was a dog but, as he got closer, he was shocked to see that it was an elf. He got out of the truck and walked closer.

Dad said, "He was pretty scared. I asked him, 'Are you alright, buddy?' He started to cry and said his leg hurt terribly. I told him not to worry; I'd help him. I scooped him up and brushed off the snow, and then I took him to Doc Morrison. The doctor was shocked to see us at the door. He said to me, 'Jimmy, I have never seen an elf before! I hope I have small enough bandages for him.' The elf liked Doc Morrison. He stopped crying and let the doc put a cast on his leg."

ANNE BARDSLEY

I had so many questions. "Where did he come from? How big was he? What was he wearing? Why didn't you wake me?"

"I did try to wake you. You wouldn't wake up. You didn't even feel him kiss your cheek."

This was too much for me! "I've been kissed by an elf?" Wait until the girls at school find out!

Dad continued to weave his tale. "Blitzen must have leaned too far to the left, and the elf just slipped off. I guess Blitzen didn't notice and kept on flying with the other reindeer. The poor little guy was so scared when I found him."

Mom suggested that we open some presents and talk more about the elf at breakfast. As she cooked the bacon and French toast, Dad told us how his new buddy, Elfie, had ridden on our dog, Towzer.

"Dad," I said, "Elves don't ride on dogs."

"Well, this one did. Towzer kept licking his nose and Elfie would laugh. Then he had some tea and cookies. He loved Snickerdoodles! Blitzen came back for him at two in the morning. I heard tapping on the window and was really surprised to see a big reindeer. His antlers were huge! Elfie was so happy to see him. I helped him back up onto Blitzen. He gave me a big hug and said, 'Thank you, Jimmy. I'll try to stop by again next Christmas. You have yourself a Merry Christmas.'"

Later that afternoon, my dad was nearly asleep on the couch with the Christmas lights twinkling. I leaned over the top of his head so we had upside down faces. I kissed his forehead and whispered, "Dad, this was the best Christmas of my whole life."

He smiled and said, "Mine too, Anne. Mine too."

Some gifts you just can't buy in a store or online.

Merry Christmas to all!

P.S. This tradition has continued with all of my sisters and with our kids. Every Christmas Eve, we buy a big bag of confectioners' sugar, dip a doll's foot in it, and replicate the footprints through our homes. We want to treasure the memory of our dad and his buddy, Elfie, from so many years ago.

My dad is smiling in heaven every Christmas Eve, I'm sure.

Memory Lane

When I was a child I cried every time we got a new car. It wasn't that I didn't like the new car; I just couldn't bear to let the old one go.

I'd beg, "Dad, we went to the Jersey shore for vacation every year in her (it was a female car). Can't we keep her and buy a new one, too?"

As my three sisters sang in the back seat, I'd stare out the back window as the car dealer drove our old car away.

My dad never understood my affection for inanimate objects. Now, years later, my daughter, Jamie, needs to trade in her beloved 1990 convertible VW Cabriolet named Lily.

That's when my drive down Memory Lane began.

Lily had been making horrible screeching noises, reminiscent of cats in heat. It was time to replace the car. Jamie bit her lip and got tears in her eyes at the mention of another car.

My husband started his, "It's time to be an adult and get a reliable car," speech for the hundredth time.

"But, Dad, just a few more dollars and I know she'll be good as new."

Unfortunately, she'd made the mistake of adding up her repair bills for Lily and telling him that it was just shy of $6,000.

My husband held firm. "No, Jamie, it's time!"

Our first trip to a used car lot brought exciting choices. Lo and behold! Right in the front row was a 2004 hunter green Cabriolet convertible. My daughter was convinced it was a sign.

The test drive went well, and she was excited about driving the new nameless car. The air conditioning ran smooth and cool. It had a great sound system. The salesman, Bill, was spouting details about the gas mileage, the new treads on the tires, and a full warranty.

"What about a trade-in?" Jamie asked.

Bill rubbed his chin. "I think I can get you one hundred dollars."

That's when things went sour.

"One hundred dollars? Are you kidding me? She has more sentimental value than that!"

Her arms were flailing now, and poor Bill was looking at my husband for support.

"I drove that bug to high school and college and grad school. Do you know the memories I have with that car?"

Bill started to stutter and backed up. "Maybe I can talk to the manager," he offered. He disappeared for a few minutes and came back with a new offer of $125.

Jamie burst into tears.

Being the mature adult that I am, I immediately put on my sunglasses because my eyes were starting to sting. I was missing Lily already. She was like a weathered friend. This was the car that Jamie had entrusted us to keep watch over when she was in Ireland for a semester. She'd call home to ask how Lily was doing. We had promised that we would car-sit Lily and take her for weekly rides to keep her in good condition (so to speak).

My husband wrenched his back weekly to keep that promise by trying to squeeze into the seat that was stuck on a setting to fit a leprechaun.

The big day came to pick up the new car. There it was! It was polished, detailed, and ready to go. Sunbeams were dancing on the hood. The dealership had it lined up, front and center, a nameless beauty. And that was just where it would stay. Jamie was not ready to let Lily go just yet.

I am proud to report that Lily is still part of our family. She has a new coat of wax, and the engine purrs like a kitten. My daughter is driving off now, with her hair blowing in the wind.

There's a smile on her face as the horn beep-beeps goodbye. I am swelling with pride!

Oh, Those Seven Pounds

Last summer I gained seven pounds.

Not eight or ten, just seven. It made such a difference though.

I am five-foot-seven inches, so a few pounds don't usually affect me. But this time, whoa!

These seven pounds were like nothing I'd ever gained before.

I didn't fret about it. I smiled more. I felt more alive. I noticed little creatures such as caterpillars and tree frogs. I even found a ladybug. I haven't seen one of those since I was a kid. In fact, I thought they might be extinct.

These seven pounds put life in perspective for me. I noticed that life moves too fast. I turned it down a notch. I started taking naps. They are delightful!

I went out for ice cream—and not just vanilla. I got double scoops of strawberry cheesecake!

I stopped at kids' lemonade stands and told them it was the best lemonade I've ever had in my life. I even bought seconds just to see them smile.

The change wrought by those seven pounds was a revelation, it was enlightenment. I had my *a-ha* moment.

My great awakening opened my eyes, my heart, and my soul.

I'm so happy with my gain that I'd like to introduce those seven pounds to you. Her name is Kaylee Elizabeth Keen and she was seven pounds at birth.

I am smitten! All I want to do is smooch her! She is precious!

Seven pounds never looked so good!

My Easter Flowers

aster has always been one of my favorite holidays. After a cold winter, the warmth of spring is truly welcome. The sight of flowers blooming reawakens my soul.

One particular Easter, I got quite the surprise. Scott took the kids out to buy me Easter flowers. I enjoyed the time at home, reading the paper and sipping coffee in peace.

Shortly, they enthusiastically arrived with my gift. The girls chattered as they walked in the door. "Oh, Mom is going to love this! They are so beautiful!"

They marched into the house like Medal of Honor recipients. Scott followed the troops and they led me to the front porch. I had no idea what to expect. Did they buy tulips, lilies, or daffodils? He had me close my eyes and guided me out the front door. When I opened my eyes, I was definitely surprised!

There on the front porch stood a two-and-a-half-foot cross wrapped in yellow ribbon. There were purple and white silk flowers flowing from the center. It had a stand behind it with metal legs to push into the grass.

He'd bought me a cemetery cross! He had no idea that it belonged on plot number 216 at St. Joseph's Cemetery. "Anne, look at this," he said proudly. "It's perfect for out back near the deck. The best thing is you can pick it up and carry it to wherever you are sitting."

I didn't have the heart to tell him the truth, so I just smiled and agreed that this was a perfect Easter present. "I never would have thought of this myself," I said honestly.

The kids clapped their hands and bounced with excitement. They were thrilled that I loved my gift.

When my parents came over, Scott showed them my new flowers and they also agreed they were lovely.

I signaled them to be quiet and not to laugh aloud. Sitting in the family room after dinner, Scott sent the kids out to bring the flowers in so we could enjoy them. They had a place of honor near the fireplace. My dad spoke first. "Scott, where did you find these? I have to get Bette some next year."

Scott told my dad that they must be very popular because there were about fifty to choose from.

My mom smiled and agreed that they looked so real, you'd never know they were silk. "It's like having a portable garden," she said as Scott proudly bent the green leaves upward for the full effect.

"Can't you just almost smell their fragrance?" I asked my mom.

"Jimmy, I hope you remember this for me next Easter," she said as Scott puffed his chest out proudly once again.

A few months later, we had to attend a funeral and that's when Scott noticed the flowers at another gravesite. He nudged me and asked, "Did you see those flowers? They look just like your Easter flowers!"

Again, I didn't have the heart to tell him. They not only looked like my flowers, they were identical!

I leaned in and whispered, "Mine are so much prettier. They're nothing like those."

He smiled proudly. I love this man!

Puppy Training

watched the *Dog Whisperer* on TV yesterday. Caesar has such command with those unruly dogs. I was seriously impressed. He discussed how important it is to train the family dog. The people are the alphas in the house.

I sipped my coffee and agreed. I looked at Miss Mattie and Mr. Murphy, my Cockapoos, and in my most authoritative voice said, "Do you hear that? I am in charge." Murphy ran off and came back with a pen in his mouth. That's when it dawned on me. Murphy is in charge.

I've been well trained by Murphy. It must have happened very slowly, because I hadn't noticed that I was being trained. This is not to say that I'm a slow learner.

Murphy seems quite happy with my performance. All he has to do is scour the house and find a pen. He then brings it to my feet and crunches it loudly to get my attention. When I attempt to take it away, the fun begins.

He snarls, shakes his head, and his jaws of steel do not open to release. After a few minutes of this, I run to the cabinet where I keep the dog treats and he follows. "Drop the pen and get a treat," I say.

Mattie also comes along barking with glee. It's as if she's cheering him on. "You got her again, Murphy! Good job!"

The pen remains in his teeth until he can actually feel the treat on the tip of his nose. Only then does he spit the pen out at my feet. He literally spits it out like a kid who had just taken medicine. "Patooey!"

I thought I had developed a genius way to get the pen away until I realized that we have only two pens left in the house. We are also very low on dog treats.

Last week, I decided this was ridiculous. The Dog Whisperer would be horrified. I need to flip flop this training. Murphy grabbed a pen and, naturally, he came right to my feet, chomping noisily. I ignored him. He stood on his hind legs so I could see him better.

Again, I pretended I didn't see or hear him. He did a few pirouettes to get my attention. Out of frustration, I grabbed for the pen only to see him take off into the other room with it still in his mouth.

Mattie was now running to the treat cabinet. I'm an equal opportunity dog-treater and she knows it. Still, I held firm.

Murphy came back and spit the pen at my feet. Before I could pick it up, he had once again clenched it in his teeth and galloped into the other room. This went on for twenty minutes.

The phone rang and I needed to write down a number to call back. "Hold on, I have to get a dog treat," I told the caller.

"What?"

I repeated, "I have to get a dog treat."

"Can you just take my number first?" the caller asked.

I was too embarrassed to tell him that I was trying to do just that. "Murphy, bring that pen over here! I'll give you a treat." He came closer, waiting to feel the beefy treat on his nose.

He spit the pen out. "Patooey!" Both dogs ran off happily with bones while I wrote the number down with yet another severely deformed, slobbery pen.

I think I'm too far gone for even the Dog Whisperer's help now.

Artsy Jamie

Jamie is my fourth child. She is extremely artsy, with a master's degree in ceramics. She has been artsy since she was a child. If anything sparkled, she loved it. The more glitter, the better.

At three, she decided to dress herself. Her outfits didn't always match, but she was colorful. I never feared losing her in a crowd.

She even had to have multi-colored sprinkles on her ice cream cones. When she was four, one of her favorite things was a trip to the drug store, just the two of us, to buy press-on fingernails. That was the highlight of her world. Naturally, the nail polish had to be bright and sparkly. This is very ironic because now that she is a ceramic artist, she must keep her nails practical and short.

At twelve, she drew a mural on her bedroom walls of her favorite people and things. When she'd get angry with one of her friends, she'd draw over that friend's name.

I figured we could always paint the walls later. Madonna influenced our decision with her song, "Express Yourself." Names would come, go, and reappear as the mural got bigger and bigger. It helped that she was artistic and could paint beautifully, or I'd have really lost my mind.

At fourteen, she came downstairs with deep red hair. She promised, "The dye will wash out in two weeks." It didn't. I was still fuming about that when she showed me her brand new belly ring. Her naval was pink and looked painfully inflamed and infected.

"Jamie, you need ointment on that right away. What were you thinking?" Then she told me it was fake. She'd been pinching her bellybutton to make it look like a real piercing.

A few days later, my mom came for Thanksgiving dinner and Jamie couldn't wait to see her reaction. Jamie met her at the door and said, "Nan, look at my new belly ring!"

Mom looked at me and grinned. "Jamie, this is perfect! Just in time for Christmas! You can hang ornaments from there. What a great idea! Maybe I could get one. Oh, and I love your red hair."

I shot my mom a look.

Jamie smiled with pride. "Nan is so cool," she said to me as she made a face.

Another time she wanted a Kurt Cobain CD. The title was *Moist Vagina*. We had a huge fight in a music store because I refused to buy her anything with a name like that. The boy behind the counter said, "Ma'am, *Moist Vagina* is really a good CD. You might like the tunes."

I was flabbergasted! He couldn't have been older than fifteen. "Young man, you are too young to even say those words!" I stormed out of the store.

Jamie suggested that Nan would buy it, since she was cool. She called Nan when we got home, and I could hear my mom on the other end of the phone shrieking, "Moist what?"

This is the same woman who never mentioned the word vagina. It was quietly referred to as "down below."

Those words are actually best whispered.

Jamie stormed up the stairs, and I heard a lot of banging and hammering. I waited an hour to let things calm down before I went to check on her. When I got there, her bedroom door was lying in the hallway. She had replaced it with beads—lots of hanging beads. It looked like a gypsy lived in my house. I thought this was her revenge, but there was more to come.

The next day, she arrived home with a black and white puffball in her palm. Jamie was acting surprisingly very sweet. I thought she was holding a stuffed animal. When I touched it, it meowed.

"Oh, Jamie, you did not bring home a kitten!" I moaned. We had Winston, a 165-pound English Mastiff. I thought he might want to have that puffball for a snack. Within ten minutes, I loved that little creature. Besides, Jamie had found it on the side of the road, all alone (that was her story anyway).

"She had no mama to feed her, and look at that face, Mom."

I went out to buy cat food.

Jamie told her sister, "She'll need a special name. She's had a tough start in life. It should be something sweet and strong, just like her."

When I got home, the puffball was given a very special, sweet, and strong name. She was christened, "Kitty." How creative!

I often think back to those days. After Kitty had four kittens, I thought it might have been easier if I'd bought that *Moist Vagina* CD. I should have gotten one for myself, too. Word is: it has great tunes!

P.S. Jamie really is artsy. You can visit her online at Jamiebardsley.com.

ANNE BARDSLEY

Busted

My husband has always had a love of flying and is always on the hunt for gadgets related to planes. He once found a radio scanner which allowed him to hear conversations of pilots flying overhead.

This was a great find for him. However, we also discovered that it picked up our kids' cell phone calls. They were teenagers at the time, and I hated that squawk box. I didn't need to know their every thought or plan although, some days, it did come in handy.

Erika was a junior in high school when her father overheard that she planned to skip school the next day. She and two friends planned to go the mall instead. They would meet at one friend's house after her mom left for work.

The next morning, Scott said, "Have a great day at school," when she left. We drove to work and that's when the fun began. Scott pulled our mechanic, Tom, into the office.

"Want to go steal a car today?"

Tom was shocked and said, "Are you crazy? What do you think I am?" When Scott explained the car caper, Tom was onboard immediately.

They drove to the house where the girls were probably enjoying skipping school. Quietly, Tom started Erika's car and drove off. Scott followed behind him, laughing to himself all the way back to the office. They drove the car inside the shop.

About two hours later, I got a call from Erika, "Mom, my car is missing."

"Did you report it to the police?" I asked. "They'll come and do a complete investigation. The person who stole it will go to prison. You'll probably have to go with them to the station to file a full report. Do you want Dad to pick you up when you're finished?" The phone went dead.

An hour later, all three girls arrived at our office. They looked like little angels in their uniforms. One was more tearful than the next. "Mrs. B, I don't know who would have the nerve to come onto the school parking lot and take the car," Katie cried.

I sympathized, "They'll find the car. Don't worry." I acted as if I had no idea they'd skipped school.

Jess agreed as she blew her nose. Tears were streaming down her face. Erika was in Scott's office, trying to find a way to get the car back and not admit that they had cut school.

Scott was having so much fun. He even called Tom into the office and asked him for ideas on how to find the car.

Tom stood between the girls with a straight face. "Gee, I don't know who would take a car right from the school parking lot."

"That's what I said," Katie chimed in.

"We don't know, either. Do you think we should all pray to St. Anthony? He finds lost things," my daughter suggested.

"Not sure that works with automobiles," my husband remarked.

"Wait, I know. That's St. Christopher! Let's pray to both of them," she suggested, wringing her hands.

Finally, Scott told them to get snacks from the vending machine in the shop. Right next to the snacks sat the car. They were completely shocked!

"How did the car get here?" they asked in unison.

Once they realized they were busted they wanted to know how Scott knew. "I just had a funny feeling that something wasn't right this morning," he told them seriously. "Maybe I'm clairvoyant."

Now they were really upset. "You let us think the car was stolen all that time and you were the one who took it?" Erika shrieked. "So I guess you know it wasn't at school then, huh?"

"I sure do. I also know the car was in front of Jess's house this morning, not in the parking lot."

Now Jess turned pale. The floodgates opened. "Please, please, don't tell my mom. I'll be grounded for a month. Please, I'm begging."

Katie was walking in circles. "My mom is going to kill me! I even called her at lunch time to tell her Erika's car got stolen."

Scott and Tom slapped each other on the back. Tom laughed aloud. "That was great! I hope I get to do that to my daughter someday. I know she'll try this one."

Scott agreed, "Yeah, count me in!"

There were other times when the squawk box saved the day. We prevented a late night party after a football game, complete with the entire team.

Another time, we overheard the planning stages of a midnight escape at a sleepover. Then there was my personal favorite, the time my daughter invited a forbidden date over to the house when she thought we'd gone away.

Her face was priceless when we walked in the door and found them kissing on the couch.

Come to think about it, I loved that old squawk box!

Chicken Pox

When my five kids were young, a trip to the store by myself or to the mailbox, for that matter, was a real treat. It was delightful not to have the three smallest bodies attached to my leg. I felt like the Hunchback of Notre Dame at times. I'd put my right foot forward, bend at the waist, and drag my left leg with the three-year-old, the two-year-old, and the one-year-old all attached. I had firm thighs back then, thanks to the additional weight I always carried around. So when my husband suggested that I go grocery shopping alone, it was like the best gift in the world. I should have known better.

When I returned home with a car full of groceries, the three younger kids were jumping up and down in the kitchen. They had their shirts pulled up to their necks and were enjoying this dance. My husband would instruct them to rest a minute and start all over again.

"What in the heck are you doing?" I asked as I made my way, bags in tow, through the jumping bodies.

"Shhh," he whispered, "I don't want to scare them. I think they have bugs. There are marks all over their stomachs and I'm trying to shake the bugs off."

I shook my head to clear out the cobwebs of what he had just said. Meanwhile, he had the broom in one hand and bug spray in the other. He was completely prepared in case a bug dropped. They continued jumping while I put the frozen food away. The older two boys just grinned, watching this from the family room.

"Take a break now, and let me see your bellies," I said. One by one, they lined up as if it was a military inspection. Sure enough, they did have little red marks on their bellies and backs.

"See if you can find any bugs," my husband said. The three of them stood there, red-bellied, sweating, and puffing for air.

The oldest reported, "Dad said we got bugs."

"Baby bugs," the other two chimed in, "with baby teeth."

By now, they really believed that there were bugs somewhere on their bodies with baby teeth, just chomping away at them.

"Dear Lord," I said to my husband, "they have chicken pox!"

He looked at me as if I was joking. "Anne, I know a bug bite when I see one."

"Put the broom and bug spray down, and go get some calamine lotion," I ordered.

After that, I decided it was probably best if I did my Hunchback impersonation rather than leave the kids with Dad.

After a few months, I'd forgotten the bug incident and left the kids with him at home again. When I returned from the drug store (no, not drugs for me, as you might suspect!) my daughters rushed to meet me at the door. "What did you bring us? Press-on nails with sparkles? Candy?"

While they fussed over the few little things for them in the bag, I settled down with a cup of tea. That's when it started.

ANNE BARDSLEY

"Mom, guess what me and Jamie have," said my three year old daughter, Erika.

So I'm guessing: candy, toys, M&Ms, and so on.

"Nope," she reported proudly. "Me and Jamie have a crotch!" She puffed out her chest.

Jamie was so excited she could barely contain herself. She had a huge smile and pointed to show me where this newly named body part was. The two girls were jumping and giddy with this newfound information.

"Woo-hoo! A crotch ... two crotches ... one for each of us!"

It was like Christmas morning without the tree.

I looked at my husband. He shrugged and said, "They said their brother has a penis. They wanted to know what they had since their penises were missing. So I had to think fast. The first thing that came to my mind was a crotch."

I may never leave the house again.

False Alarm

Scott and I have been married for thirty-five years. In those years, humor has kept our marriage alive and strong. Trust me. I speak from experience. I'll give you a little peek into my world.

Last year, we got a new alarm system. I was afraid of the panel and never touched it. Scott, on the other hand, likes to know how things work. One night, I went to bed early. I never do that but, on this night, I was the kind of tired to where you just can't do one more thing. I slipped into my wrinkled, oversized birthday suit and was asleep in seconds.

I was awakened by Scott screaming, "Anne, get up! Get up! The firemen are coming!"

I blinked my eyes and asked, "Do we have a fire?"

"No! Just get up!"

I told him, "No fire; Anne is not getting up."

I heard him on the phone in the next room, yelling random words as if he had Tourette syndrome. He was talking to the alarm company and trying to remember our password.

He ran back into the room, and I pretended to be asleep.

"Get up! You have to entertain the firemen!" he started screaming.

"There is no fire … what firemen?" And how am I supposed to entertain firemen, anyway? It's not as if I had a pole in my living room to slide down.

I heard sirens coming down the street. They were getting louder and louder. Lights flashed in the window. Our dog, Murphy, howled in tune to the sirens.

"Stop that howling, Murphy," Scott bellowed.

The woman on the phone from the alarm company apparently felt so badly for Scott she gave him a password hint. It begins with the letter 'M.'

He began pacing and shouting into the phone, "Mary, Mona, mayo, Martha, Mother of God … I don't know!" Murphy continued to howl. "Can you hold on a minute, please?" he asked the woman. "Murphy, shut up!" he yelled.

The woman asked, "What was that you said? I thought I heard the password."

"No, I was just telling the dog to be quiet."

There was a bang on the door and, by then, I was awake and dressed.

The fireman at the door was wearing a HUGE helmet with a light like they use at the gynecologist's office. I immediately started cramping. He was holding an axe and dressed in full fireman regalia. Our other dog, Mattie, saw this humongous creature at our door, backed up, and proceeded to pee on the floor.

Scott told the fireman that he was so sorry. He had just tried to adjust the alarm. "It will never happen again," he swore.

Murphy was still howling.

The firemen got back in the truck and drove down the street. Scott reset the alarm and I heard a huge sigh. I headed back to bed and back into my oversized, wrinkled birthday suit. My head hit the pillow, and I could feel sleep coming on.

Just then, the phone rang. It was the alarm company. Scott hit the wrong button and now they thought we had a burglar. The police had been alerted. They needed our password.

Here we go again.

"Mona, Mary, mayo," I could hear him saying, "For the love of God!"

I yelled, "It's the dog's name … Murphy!"

What does a girl have to do to get some sleep in this house?

ANNE BARDSLEY

Codependency

I was very upset when I found out I was a "codependent."

I remember thinking, "I'm just a very nice person. I will take care of you whether you need it or not." There is nothing wrong with that, *is there?*

The nuns in school told us that we should turn the other cheek if someone hurt us. It was very important to be nice. Well, someone should have had a little chat with those sisters.

When I realized that all that niceness wasn't necessarily a healthy thing, I looked for a support group to fix my condition. I found a six-week course. We met every Monday night from eight to ten.

There were eight women in our group, and I'd have to say that the other seven were serious co-deps. I was glad I wasn't as bad as they were. Whew! Talk about issues! I felt healthier almost immediately.

I seem to have a gift. I can do emotions for someone else. If they're smiling, but inside they're crying, I can sense their tears and cry for them. It's very strange.

I thought this was incredibly sensitive of me until the psychologist who moderated our group explained that I am definitely a co-dep. I can do other people's feelings better than my own! What a revelation this turned out to be! So I went back every week and, little by little, I noticed that I was like those other women.

The six weeks were nearly over and our group was due to end, but the psychologist suggested we go a little longer. And so we did. Our six-week codependency group lasted five years!

I'm so glad I'm healthier now, but I think that psychologist has severe co-dep issues.

She just couldn't say goodbye to us.

I could just cry for her.

Going Buggy

My sister, Mary, is eight years younger than me. She has three daughters. The last one came as a surprise when she was forty. Well, a shock might be more honest.

If I had to describe Mary, I'd say that she has very good taste in fashion and beauty products. She always looks great. She has a dry sense of humor, is a vegan, and a clean freak. She showers twice a day. Mary is pretty much immaculate—no Catholic joke intended.

Last month she called in a panic and said her daughter had come home from vacation with bugs. Mary was horrified ... she believed they were bed bugs. She'd already called the hotel where they had stayed to complain. She told me that she was treating them like lice and that they should be gone soon.

A week went by and she called again to tell me that her other daughter was now infected. Their doctor examined the girls' hair and couldn't find a thing. In fact, he suggested she might want to see a psychologist for this unnatural fear of bed bugs. Mary stormed out of his office.

A few days later, she called again and told me that she now had these damned bugs, and they were infecting her house.

She sprayed and bought a dozen bottles of lice medicine, but they were still multiplying. My scalp began to itch.

She had taken to wearing a shower cap around the house so the bugs wouldn't jump on the furniture. In fact, all of the girls were wearing shower caps. She tried to get one on the dog, but he chewed it off. Her husband insisted there were no bugs. This just infuriated her.

Another week went by. When I called to check on things, she said they now had a plan to get rid of the bed bugs once and for all. As she told me this, I could hear the plastic shower cap crackling.

"Are you still wearing those shower caps?"

"Of course!" she said. "I can't let them get on the furniture and carpets. They'll be breeding in my Berber!" I checked my own carpet for creatures.

Her family had developed a routine. Every day, they got in the shower and rinsed any stray bugs away. Next, they put the anti-bug treatment in their hair. While it worked, they scoured the area for baby eggs. Next, she yelled to her daughter, "Take those clothes off. We have to boil them. Get the sheets off your bed, too."

Half laughing, I asked, "Mary, you're boiling clothes?"

"Of course!" she said seriously. "I have a big pot on the stove. I call it my cauldron. I will get these damned bugs out of my house one way or another." Her husband still insisted there were no bugs.

Next, she told me that she captured one in a Ziploc bag and took it to the exterminator to identify it and find out how to kill it. She and her two daughters had piled into the car with the dead bug in a bag and their shower caps in place.

When they arrived at the pest control office, the man was quite surprised to see them in their shower caps, but he was very pleasant. He reported, "It's definitely a beetle's wing you have there."

Well, that did not sit well with Mary. She had already checked things out on a bug and insect website. The mini comb that came in the package of lice hair treatment was supposed to collect the little bug larvae, but she knew it was not doing the trick.

There was more to this infestation than met the eye. She had seen them under a magnifying glass with her own eyes. They were nasty critters and she wanted some real answers.

She was confident that it was at least a bed bug, surely not a beetle's wing. "Beetle wings don't chew your scalp!" she snarled.

She offered to remove her shower cap and let him see them in action on her head, but he declined the offer.

Her husband, John, screamed, "If I hear one more thing about these damn bugs, I'm going to leave the state. And get the plastic sheets off our bed! We've spent hundreds of dollars trying to get rid of them, and I'm sick and tired of it. For God's sake, Mary, you even shaved the dog! The water bill has tripled! For the last time, there are no bugs! You're hallucinating!"

He left the house in a tie-dyed button-down that used to be one of his favorite blue shirts prior to the cauldron.

Not to be deterred, Mary visited an entomologist at the University of Georgia with the Ziploc bag in hand. She was going to get to the bottom of this once and for all. She promised John this would be her final attempt to find a cure for this madness.

The entomologist was very understanding. He sympathized with Mary's frustration. He removed the dead bug, slipped it under a microscope, and looked at it for a long time. Then he said, "This is very interesting. How long have you been scratching and doing treatments?"

Mary was ecstatic that someone was taking the situation seriously. "About six weeks," she reported. She breathed a sigh of relief that, finally, the mystery bug would be identified. It was worth the hour drive to meet this very intelligent professor. At last, she could get rid of the varmints.

"Well, Mary," he said, "this is indeed a beetle's wing. It has no teeth and it can't breed. You have phantom bug syndrome."

She sat with her mouth wide open in disbelief and scratched her head.

I was so relieved to hear the news. Every time I had talked to her about these bugs, I swore I was getting bitten. I was on high-alert bug watch.

Her husband is happy. The dog's fur has grown in. The shower caps are long gone. The cauldron is now a soup pot. Life at their house is good again.

She called yesterday and during our conversation she said, "Hold on, Anne. I think I see ants on my kitchen counter."

I hung up the phone and went out to buy ant traps.

Gotcha

When my son, Michael, was about fifteen, the rebellion began. He started smoking pot. His grades dropped.

The school suggested a new thirty-day residential treatment program to get him back on track. It would work on his self-confidence and stressed personal responsibility. Michael did quite well in the program.

The facility was in the middle of the woods in the Pocono Mountains surrounded by big oak trees. They saw hawks, eagles, sparrows ... you name it. It was a nature wonderland! The air was crisp, the trees were changing colors; it was breathtaking!

The minister told them, "If there is a Higher Power, let a bird fly by the window in the next five minutes." They waited, with no bird in sight. "Well, let's give it a few more minutes," he said hopefully. Again, not a bird in sight. The class ended without a bird sighting. So much for a Higher Power, *right*?

The next day, they met once again with the minister. They had all forgotten about the bird by then. The minister opened the window for some fresh air. That's when it happened!

A bird flew in the window. It circled the class at head level, wings flapping wildly. Michael put up his hand and the bird perched on his finger.

"It was unbelievable!" he said. "It looked me right in the eye and chirped at me! Now, what are the chances of that happening?"

Not a single person who was there could deny the circling feathered friend and the presence of a Higher Power that day.

I often think of that story. Sometimes when you need a sign, you want it right now. This time, it seemed that the Higher Power had a sense of humor.

I bet he shouted, "Gotcha!" to the nonbelievers.

Contrary Attraction

We've all heard the old wives tale about how, after many years of marriage, husbands and wives start to look and act like each other. With us, it's more like opposites attract, and we couldn't be more different.

Scott shaves his head and he has suggested that I do the same. He thinks that I should buy an assortment of wigs, just because I complain about my hair daily ... okay, sometimes hourly.

Scott has muscular legs and thighs. He loves to work out at the gym until he's dripping with sweat and breathless.

I prefer to watch workout videos with a big fan blowing on me while I munch from a huge bowl of corn chips (baked, naturally). Muscular legs and thighs are on my wish list, but not on my to-do list.

Scott is calm and centered. He wakes slowly, reads the morning paper quietly, and sips his decaf tea.

I tend to have attention deficit disorder from the moment I open my eyes. I'm very serious when I tell you that within two minutes of being awake, I have a minimum of twenty-five things that have already crossed my mind. Thanks to menopause, I can't remember them, but I know they were there because I'm exhausted just thinking of all the things I have to get done.

When he asked me to sit down and make a list to simplify my day, here's what I came up with that made me so exhausted: 1) call the dog groomer and 2) grocery shop.

That's it! The twenty-five things that first overwhelmed me before I even sat up have gone into the back of my mind. Once they get there, there's no telling when they'll resurface!

My husband writes only in black ink, and he actually has a book where he notes all the passwords for his different accounts.

I once wrote in it with a different pen, and used all lower case letters. He had a fit! "Anne, seriously. Use black ink and write in all upper case." I am not allowed to touch that book anymore. It seems he's not fond of cursive or purple ink.

I also have a book for my passwords, but I can't read half of what I write. It's a very colorful book, by the way. Black ink can be so dull.

There are green, purple, and blue notes, and not necessarily in the appropriate little boxes. I also have my own personal filing system. The City of St. Petersburg water bill is filed under "W" for water. The Bright House bill is filed under "C" for cable. It wasn't until he couldn't locate the Kohl's bill that we had a real problem.

"Where in the name of God did you put the Kohl's statement?" he asked.

"The Kohl's bill is filed under "D" to remind myself, don't charge more there." It makes perfect sense to me. When he finds the "D" file (my "Don't" file), he also comes across a Chinese restaurant menu, a sales ad that expired months ago, and a note on which I'd written my new goal from 2010: "Get Organized Now!" I may need to make an "F" file for "Forget It!"

I recently realized that most of my time at home is spent closing cabinet doors and putting away the things that he leaves out. It's as if he grew up in a house of royalty and had a butler to follow him as a child.

Just this morning, he got a mug out for coffee and left the door open. Then he got the sugar bowl down from the cabinet and left that door open. Next, he went for a spoon and left that drawer open. After I banged my head on the sugar bowl cabinet door, I yelled, "Can't you just close one cabinet door?"

"Door? What door?" he asked with a puzzled look on his face. I feel like Vanna White without the gown, only I close doors instead of moving big letters.

Now, if I ever forget to close a cabinet anywhere, he calls me from wherever I am in the house to come and see it immediately. He calls me with such alarm in his voice, I assume it's an emergency.

"Aha!" he chirps like a Colombo impersonator. "What is this I see, Anne? An open door?"

Naturally, I respond, "Vanna doesn't do doors! Do you want to buy a vowel?"

Maverick is in the House

knew my husband had watched the movie *Top Gun* too many times when our four-year-old, Justin, took on a new personality.

He asked his nursery school teacher, "Can you call me Mav? It's short for Maverick."

When he went to the grocery store with my mom and noticed all the ladies in the store, he told her, "Nan, this is a target-rich environment."

I would call him in for dinner and he'd yell back, "Negative, Ghost Rider, the pattern is full."

One morning at breakfast he told Scott, "I feel the need ... the need for speed!" Where did my four-year-old go?

When I heard him yelling in his room, I rushed upstairs to hear, "I'm hit! I'm hit! Viper, they're on my tail!" He was seriously in movie mode.

His sisters complained that he was annoying. Jamie moaned, "My friends were here, and he ran into my room asking, 'Any of you guys seen an aircraft carrier around here?' This is ridiculous! Then he flew out of the room like a jet, yelling something about having tone!"

I vowed to have Scott talk to him.

When Scott came home I told him about Maverick, I mean Justin.

He laughed until Justin came by, and said, "Hey, Dad, this is Ghost Rider one-one-seven. This bogey is all over me. Do I have permission to fire?"

Scott looked at me, "Maybe I shouldn't have let him watch the movie with me so many times." He reasoned with Justin, "*Top Gun* is only a movie."

Justin responded, "Son, your ego is writing checks your body can't cash."

Scott sat in the chair and rubbed his forehead. A few minutes later, Justin buzzed by saying, "Slider, you stink!"

When my dad came over, Justin asked, "Hey, Pop, do you want to buzz the tower?"

My dad asked, "What tower?"

Justin had to think about it. He changed the subject. "I'm going to need something to put these flames out."

Pop shook his head. "Hey, Justin, let's go buzz that tower."

They were getting in my dad's truck when I heard Justin say, "I want some butts, and I want them now!"

My dad laughed and said, "Hey, Mav, put on your seatbelt. Got your parachute?"

"Yes, sir! Maverick signing off!" he announced as he saluted.

The fascination with flight never left Justin. As a teenager, he finally had a need for a parachute when he went skydiving. Though he never flew a jet off the deck of an aircraft carrier, he loved to soar in the sky, and he even took a few flying lessons.

There was just something about a military man that made me proud—even if he was only four.

Professionalism

Scott and I had our own business in Pennsylvania. I was in charge of sales. At eight-and-one-half months pregnant, I scheduled a sales call against my better judgment. I probably should have stayed home that day. I have my mom's work ethic, however, so I drove an hour away to call on this customer.

The offices were on the second floor. I lugged my forty-pound stomach up the twisting stairs and arrived panting. The receptionist was very sweet. Her expression was pure shock. "Oh my! Look at you!" She must have thought that I was about to explode any second. She rushed to get me a glass of water. I relaxed, sank into the leather sofa, and took deep breaths.

Within a few minutes, a small-framed man entered the waiting room and introduced himself as Joe Forester. He made me feel at ease right away. He was exceptionally pleasant and had a warm smile. "Let's go back to my office," he said.

I gathered my purse and sales binder. "Great, let's go!" I said eagerly. I leaned forward and realized that I was stuck in the sofa. I tried a few more lunges forward, but my baby bump was so large, I couldn't get any leverage. I had become part of the seat beneath me.

With all the lunging, I'd awoken the sleeping giant in my belly. He kicked and stretched in what looked like a bull trying to escape a rodeo ring. My doctor had warned me to call immediately when labor started because he was sure there was one very large baby in my belly. He guessed close to ten pounds. My belly was so tight that you couldn't miss the bumps from his gymnastics.

I was so embarrassed! I could feel tears forming. One-hundred-fifty pound Joe gave me his hand and just braced himself for my weight.

On the first try, he gave a mighty tug. I rose up an inch and fell back, pulling Joe on top of me in a tangle. With a flustered look on his face, he righted himself, and braced again. On the second try, we met in the middle. I raised a foot off the sofa, but I was still far from upright. He was ready for me to fall back and managed to keep his feet. On the third try, I was vertical!

Belly now in full motion, we walked into his office. I leaned on a filing cabinet, afraid to take a seat as he suggested. I stood there blowing puffs at my sweaty bangs.

Unlike my bambino, I was not interested in any type of exertion, let alone gymnastics.

Finally, things settled down in the mid-section.

I got the account! Joe walked with me as I waddled happily out of his office and back down the winding stairs.

Over the years, we often laughed about that day. "You know, you definitely made a lasting impression."

Over many lunches, we'd embellish the story to the point where we'd be in hysterics. I was so sorry when he passed.

He was my favorite customer for over thirty years.

Sometimes you don't need to be perfectly professional. You just have to be real … and that's good enough.

ANNE BARDSLEY

Two Old Gals Gone Wild

Nancie and I have been friends since we were in diapers. She is older than me by two weeks. I've never let her forget that.

"Nancie, since you are my elder, I expect you to be a good example for me to follow."

She sipped her wine and grinned. Although we've been friends for over fifty years, I never knew how different we were until we spent a week together on St. John, US Virgin Islands.

It was a two-old-gals getaway. That's when I realized that she is organized, hyper-vigilant, driven, energetic, and athletic ... and I am not.

We arrived at The Hummingbird Cottage. It was located at the top of what would have been a triple black diamond slope had it been covered in snow.

If I didn't lean forward walking up the hill, I was in serious danger of rolling back down (who am I kidding? I coughed, sweated, and damn near needed a T-bar). The cottage was lovely, surrounded by flowers and tropical trees full of singing birds. In the distance, steel drum music played.

We settled in, and that's when I noticed Nancie's organizational skills far surpassed mine. I emptied my luggage in three minutes flat—Nancie took fifteen. When I went to see what was taking her so long, I was amazed.

When she opened her closet, everything was perfectly coordinated. Her outfits were hanging on hangers without a single wrinkle and arranged by color from light yellow to a dark blue in rainbow sequence. On her dresser she laid out seven pairs of earrings and seven necklaces in the same color sequence.

When she asked to see what I brought, I said ashamedly, "Well, I brought three bathing suits. They're all stuffed in the top drawer. I also have three tops and three pairs of shorts but none match."

She was horrified. "Annie, where's your jewelry?" she asked sadly.

"I'm wearing it," I told her.

"Annie, they don't even match what you're wearing now! We'll have to go shopping." She left the room and I heard her sigh, "Oh, poor Annie."

Nancie is very curious about the world, and she is able to retain facts like an encyclopedia.

I sat on the private veranda and watched a beautiful hummingbird hovering around the flowers that grew at the edges when she said, "A hummingbird's wings flap eighty times per second. Their little feet are not for standing, or walking—only perching. They lay one to three eggs at a time and their gestation is only thirteen to twenty-two days."

Who knew? Mental note to self: Get educated!

Each morning we'd have coffee and a muffin on the veranda. "What's the weather today?" I'd ask.

The response was, "There will be a low of 72 degrees tonight and a nice breeze today with the high temperature of 88 degrees. The island temperature doesn't vary all year round." She must have read about meteorology in the encyclopedia.

I also learned that Nancie is hyper-vigilant. At three in the morning, I awoke to someone in my room. It was Nancie, closing the windows in the middle of a thunderstorm. I had slept right through it.

She said, "Go back to sleep. I'm just going to bring in the patio furniture cushions." She has boundless energy.

The next morning we were having coffee when she yelled, "Ah-ha! I finally figured out what's wrong with the back door." She is also talented mechanically and, within minutes, she'd fixed the creak in the door. And she did all of this in matching shorts, top, necklace, earrings, and flip flops. It was our third day, so she was in coral pink.

Nancie has loved the island of St. John for years. She swears that it is her heart's home and that one day she will live there. One of the items on her bucket list was to meet Mr. Guy Benjamin, the author of *My Beloved Virgin*. He is a legend on the island.

He had dedicated his life to educating the children in St John. There is a school named in his honor. He is deeply loved and respected by the locals. When you ask anyone if they know how to contact him, the answer is always the same. "Oh, he's here on the island." No further information is given. They're very protective of his privacy.

Nancie was very disappointed that no one would give her his address, but she was not deterred. She convinced herself that somehow she would find him.

The next day we rented a jeep. We went exploring and, as we drove down a narrow, rutted dirt road, I saw a blue sign hammered together that read, "If you want to meet Mr. Benjamin, honk three times."

I said, "Did you see that sign?"

She reversed at warp speed and slammed on the brakes, almost throwing me from the open vehicle. She pounded the horn, but no sound came out. I was still recovering and grabbing my neck from the whiplash when she leaped out of the car.

She screamed, "BEEP BEEP BEEP," at the top of her lungs. Her legs were moving like Wile E. Coyote in a cartoon. Chickens scrambled away all over the yard, startled by this flapping, screeching, beeping woman.

When I got out of the car, the chickens had taken refuge under their coop. I walked up to the screen door, and saw a tall, thin black man with soft eyes and a big smile. Nancie had him in her grips! She hugged him and crooned, "Mr. Benjamin! Oh! Mr. Benjamin!"

He was so happy and enjoyed the attention.

Nancie told me to take pictures. I grabbed the 35mm camera and while I was focusing, she leaned over and whispered, "Take it from the waist up."

I was just about to ask her why when the camera came into focus on them. Mr. Benjamin had just finished his lunch, and half of a white linen napkin was sticking out of the zipper of his pants. I didn't know what to think. Maybe it was an island custom.

I snapped the picture and I must say … they were two of the happiest people on the island. He told us he was ninety-six and loved having visitors.

He offered to give Nancie a copy of his book, *My Beloved Virgin*, for the reduced price of twenty dollars. She was ecstatic when he signed the book and wrote a little note. It was as if she'd won the lottery.

The next day, we went on a kayaking/snorkeling/walking tour that she had scheduled. We kayaked to a nearby smaller island. Nancie jumped out of the kayak like a gazelle. I tumbled into the water, made a big splash, screamed, and gulped salt water. She snorkeled off like a pro. I had my mask on upside-down and almost choked to death.

I did get to see a large sea turtle swim by me. He was probably trying to sleep, and I woke him up with all my coughing.

I kept a journal on this trip so that I'd be able to remember all of our adventures when we're ninety.

When we got back to the cottage, I wrote, "On our tour, we learned about a crab who lives on the island. He's a horny little creature who will roll down the mountain looking for love. He will then hump another crab and begin his trek back up the mountain. I think there may be horny toad frogs that do the same. It must be something about the tropics that puts love in the air."

Nancie's version was, "The soldier crab is like a living barometer—it can predict storms. He knows when to head to higher ground. He will roll himself down the mountain to mate and then he climbs all the way back up. In the old days, the weather was predicted by the location of these soldier crabs."

I think I need to pay more attention. Again, I say, "Encyclopedia."

On our last day there, we sat downtown listening to steel drums playing a calypso. The ferry had arrived and people were coming and going. The breeze was just right. I looked over and saw that Nancie had tears in her eyes.

"Annie, I don't want to leave," she whispered as a tear escaped down her cheek. "This is where I belong."

I cried with her—she was so alive and happy here. I hugged her shoulder and told her, "Nanc, one day this will be your home. Let's make that happen."

She smiled and another tear let loose.

All too soon, we were headed back to reality. On the flight home, I paged through my journal. I realized that the time we had together was priceless.

Yes, she is older than me, more organized, hyper-vigilant, driven, and athletic. She has a flair for matching outfits. She remembers facts, and she can fix things … but I love her anyway.

Make Him Notice You All Over Again

"Make Him Notice You All Over Again," the ad read, inviting me to a facial rejuvenation seminar. So exciting! This sixty-year-old face would be rejuvenated. The crow's feet around my eyes would be erased. My laugh lines would disappear. With this new treatment, my face would stay firm and wrinkle free. I could barely contain myself. My husband would surely notice that my youthful beauty had returned.

When he got home, I couldn't control myself. I blurted out the news immediately. I really hoped he'd be equally enthusiastic about my rejuvenation.

"Have you noticed that my face isn't as young as it used to be?"

"No, but your legs look older to me," he replied.

"Forget my legs. I'm talking about my face."

"Your face is fine. What's for dinner?"

"Roast chicken, veggies, and a baked potato in about an hour. Now, let's talk more about my face."

"Anne," he said impatiently, "what is up with your face anyway?"

I was getting nowhere.

"Well, this ad says that you'll notice me all over again if I get the top of the line rejuvenation package." I waved the invitation in front in of him to show him the before and after pictures. Seeing is believing! "I don't like the idea of plastic surgery, but maybe you'll notice me more."

"Notice you more? How could I notice you more? There's only you and me in the house, and we see each other all the time. I notice you. Right now, I'm noticing that you're not starting dinner and I'm hungry," he grouched.

"Seriously, look at my face," I said, determined to get his full attention.

"Okay, I'm looking at your face. Can we talk about your legs now?"

"No! No leg talk! Now focus!" I barked.

I was beginning to wish I'd never brought the subject up.

"All right, let me get my glasses and I'll inspect your face if that will make you happy."

He came back with his magnifying trifocal lenses to begin his inspection. "Holy God! Look at all those hairs on your face!" he said, squinting at me.

I knew this was a bad idea. I should have asked a girlfriend.

"Which lines are you worried about?" he asked as he held my chin and turned my face from side to side.

"How many are there?" I asked.

"Do you want me to count them?"

"Lord, no! Just give me an area that you think might need some of that rejuvenation," I told him wearily.

"Well, you have lines on your forehead, cheeks, nose, and chin. You have lines at your eyes and around your mouth," he reported.

"Those are my laugh lines," I scolded. "They don't count."

"What do you mean they don't count? Am I counting lines or not?"

"Just count the big ones," I finally said.

"Those are the big ones! Do you want a line count on the little ones, too? Did I mention your wattle under your chin? Do they charge per wrinkle? You may need to ask for a payment plan."

All of this information was stressing me. Hairy face, big lines, little lines, wattles. I made a mental note to break those trifocals.

"Take off those glasses and go watch sports," I told him. He happily obliged, almost running to the TV.

During dinner, I worried about collecting the free certificate. My husband noticed me talking to myself. When I'm upset, I often have silent heart-to-heart conversations with myself, complete with facial expressions. I may look a tad demented, but I process all sorts of problems this way.

"Now I know where those lines come from. Your brow is all wrinkled up. What are you saying in there?" he asked.

"I was just thinking that even the top of the line rejuvenation wouldn't work on this many lines. I just wanted you to notice me more. If I don't get this done, who knows what I could look like next year? My face could droop right onto my chest. And then what would I look like?" I asked, not really expecting an answer.

He stopped chewing and just looked at me. "Dear God, you'd have a face between your boobs! And you thought I wouldn't notice you?"

That sent me into a fit of laughter.

"Better stop that," he said. "you're making more lines!"

I decided that he was noticing me and that laughter is the best rejuvenation.

The Fresh Smell of Spring

t had been the coldest winter in thirty years in Pennsylvania. Pipes froze. Car door locks froze. If you had a tear in your eye, that froze too. We stored water and soda in the garage and they froze.

After a month or so, we just got used to the garage being like an extra freezer. One warm day in April, that all changed.

I came home from work on a Friday afternoon and found Scott cleaning the garage. We never do this on a weekday night. It's an all-day Saturday job. As I opened my car door, a wave of the most putrid odor hit me. "What is that smell?"

"Cover your nose," Scott yelled. "Wrap something around your face so you don't get sick from the smell."

I pitched in to help him and, as we emptied out the garage, we noticed a little trickle of blood coming from a trash bag. It was beyond disgusting. It was like a horror show. Scott said, "Don't touch anything. Go buy gallons of bleach. Don't forget rubber gloves."

When I came back, I said, "Scott, you're the man. You have to open it." I backed up in fear. I had no idea what could be in that big, black bag with a tiny twisty tie. Whatever it was, it could not be good.

Scott argued, "You open it. Do I always have to do all the manly things?"

"Well, yeah. You're the man!" I held firm.

He peeked into the bag and, sure enough, it was something dead.

Just then, my son Mike came home, and the first thing he said was, "What is that horrible smell?"

Scott handed him the bag. "I think this might be yours."

Mike gulped. "Oh crap! I was going to have this deer head mounted. I forgot all about it. I guess this isn't a good time to tell you that the lizard got out of the terrarium, is it?"

At that point, I actually thought of having his head mounted and put in the family room!

It would be a great conversation piece. "Yes, that's our son, Mike, who forgot that he had left a deer head in the garage and stunk out the entire neighborhood last April. He also lost a two-foot-long lizard, named Dingo, in his bedroom. Watch where you walk, we haven't found Dingo yet."

A week later, the smell of bleach was finally fading in our garage when Mike announced that trout season started the next day.

I had visions of bags of fish in our garage, awaiting an appointment with the taxidermist.

As he gathered his bait, I yelled, "Here Dingo! Come on out. Mike is taking you to the lake. Maybe you can have a feast on all those fish he plans to catch. Road trip!"

I didn't wait to see if Dingo arrived. I went inside and called my stockbroker to invest in Clorox.

ANNE BARDSLEY

How I Earned My Wrinkles

have been blessed by the Wrinkle Fairy.

She perches on my right shoulder. I caught her waving her sparkly wrinkle wand at me last week. She was laughing as she anointed me. I frowned at her and tried to swat her away.

It's not easy avoiding the Wrinkle Fairy when you are married to the Master Wrinkle Maker ... my husband, Scott.

I noticed that the Wrinkle Fairy is more active when he is in the room. I follow him around, closing cabinet doors and drawers, putting things back in the fridge, and searching for his ever-lost keys.

He also swears that he tells me important facts, but I never remember hearing them come from his mouth. For instance, he claims that he told me, "Don't use the American Express card. The balance is getting too high."

That afternoon, I went out and charged $214 on—you guessed it—American Express. I have no recollection of his conversation about not using that card. I think he is messing with my head.

This makes me wrinkle up while I try to backtrack in my menopausal mind. I can barely remember him, let alone an imaginary conversation. The Wrinkle Fairy notices my expressions, so she does a little twirl and BAM! She shakes her wand at me

When you are raising five kids, there is always something, and someone, to worry about. I even got little blessings from the fairy back then. When they were teenagers, I'd huddle in the cold and dark at two in the morning, just waiting for them to try to sneak into the house. I'd be praying, "Dear God, please let them drive up now and be safe ... so I can personally kill them!"

The Wrinkle Fairy was not happy about being awake on a cold dark night either. She zapped me twice! BAM! BAM!

When my estrogen level plummeted, the Wrinkle Fairy worked overtime. She almost fell off my shoulder from daily fits of laughter. She got dizzy, spinning and bopping me with that wand of hers. I remember thinking that I needed to shake her off, but then I'd get busy and forget. This forgetfulness caused my crow's feet to turn into eagle's claws. My brow is so wrinkled, I look like a little puggle dog, but I'm not small enough for it to be so cute.

Yesterday, I went to the grocery store without my list. There was only one item, so I figured I could remember it easily. I went up and down every single aisle trying to remember why I made this crucial trip. I could not remember to save my life.

When I got home, I splashed water on my face, and when I looked in the mirror, I remembered ... I had gone to the store for WRINKLE CREAM! My fairy friend started doing the Macarena on my shoulder.

I made the mistake of telling Scott about this. In the middle of the night, he got up to go to the bathroom. I heard him yelling, "Get out of here! Get! Get! Don't even think about it!" I thought we must have a water bug or mosquito.

He came back to bed and I asked him what was in there.

"It was one of your wrinkles trying to attach itself to me. Don't worry, I caught it and flushed it. You're safe tonight."

Oh, for the love of … !

My fairy rolled over and covered her ears. It must be exhausting being my fairy. She needs her rest. Who knew that laughing could cause so many wrinkles?

She and I have made peace. I've decided to embrace her blessings. By the way, she told me her name is Wanda. I call her Wanda with the sparkly wrinkle wand. We are now best friends. I'm taking her to lunch today. BFF.

My Yellow Toes

Last year Scott surprised me with a pedicure for Mother's Day. It sounded very relaxing.

He said, "You don't have to do a thing. I'll even get the nail polish." I thought this sounded lovely. I remembered for a minute that he is colorblind, but quickly dismissed the thought.

When he arrived home from shopping, I asked, "What color did you pick?"

He reached into the bag and pulled out a school bus yellow bottle of polish.

"I've never seen that color before," I told him.

"Anne, it's the color of Alexander Ovechkin's skate laces. I had to buy it."

Now, I understand hockey fan loyalty, but seriously? The color of a hockey player's laces? Did he ever think Anne isn't a fan of yellow? Obviously not.

To be a good sport and to appreciate the thought behind the gift, I went along. Well, not only is he colorblind, he has horrible peripheral vision. It looked like a kindergartner finger painted my toes! I had yellow all over my cuticles.

When he offered to do my fingernails to match, I quickly replied, "Oh, no! You have done so much for me already."

I hoped no one would notice my feet, but in a state where flip flops are considered formal wear, they are out for viewing all day, every day. And believe me, people noticed. I was at the grocery store when an older lady spotted my yellow polish. "Well, aren't you bright today?" she remarked.

I explained that it was a gift from my husband. "Really?" she said as she raised her eyebrow. "Are you still married?"

I told her, "It was a very sweet gesture, and I love it."

After two weeks of remarks from strangers about my pedicure, I decided to get a color change. At the nail salon, a lady came to do my pedicure and, naturally, she asked about my Alexander Ovechkin's skate lace color polish. I told her, "My husband did this as a gift."

She burst out laughing. "Yor huband do this to yu? Ha ha ha ha!"

I tried to explain that he did it for Mother's Day, as a gift from the heart. By now, six other women were cackling, and all I could understand was, "Her huband do dat to huh, tee hee hee."

They were huddling in a fit of hysterics. One by one, they came by to inspect my feet.

"Oh, yor huband? You like your huband?" they asked and chuckled.

The owner of the salon came over to see what all the commotion was about. "Yor huband must be berry sweet. I wish my huband do dis for me."

Naturally, I picked Ovechkin's skate lace yellow for my nail polish color once again.

Husband and hockey rock!

Winston

Every family has had a pet that sets the standard for future pets. If you ask anyone in our family who our most adored pet was, the answer would be unanimous. It was our English Mastiff, Winston James of Gwynedd.

He was a huge (literally) part of our family. He was enormous in body with the mind of a small child. He could scare anyone with his bellowing bark and, in the next minute, he would be afraid of a little squeaking toy.

I drove two hours with my son, Justin, to pick up our eight-week-old puppy. The mother of the litter walked slowly to greet us at the door. I think motherhood had worn her out. She looked so tired. She just sat patiently nearby and watched us. The father of the litter was another story.

We were ushered out back to view the puppies where the owners kept them in a storage area below a raised deck. When they unlatched the door, the four pups ran in different directions. That's when we saw the papa of the brood, galloping toward us at full speed.

His huge jowls were slobbering in the wind. He must have weighed three hundred pounds and looked like the size of a pony. He was carrying a rope toy that was like something you'd use to herd cattle.

"Run for your life!" Justin screamed.

We ran for cover. All he wanted was someone to throw that twenty-pound rope toy for him. Who knew?

Deciding which puppy to bring home was very difficult for me, but one little guy tugged at my son's heart. Sure enough, he was the one we chose. We chose the name Winston, which had a regal sound.

Winston didn't move for the entire two-hour ride home. He sat perched on Justin's lap with his back legs dangling off the seat. He'd look at me, then up to Justin. I could almost hear him thinking, "Who are you people and where is my mom?"

Winston never knew that he was becoming a very large dog. He was happiest on someone's lap or right next to us on the sofa. When he was fully grown, he could fill the loveseat by himself. If my husband and I were sitting there, Winston would squeeze in between us and wiggle until he got comfortable. We would sit pressed up against the sides of the sofa, but he was happy. He'd look back and forth at us, squirming with excitement.

Although he was large and muscular at one hundred sixty-five pounds, he was skittish about the silliest things. One night, as my husband walked him up the street, the sound of the rustling fall leaves scared Winston. He walked hunched down low, shaking as if those leaves could really hurt him.

He dragged my husband home and then climbed onto the sofa next to me, panting and trembling. He was such a scaredy-cat. The next night, I found him on our back patio, jumping and doing pirouettes, trying to bite at the lightning strikes in the sky. I was soaking wet after dragging him back into the house.

Another time, I woke up at two in the morning and heard him whimpering. I went downstairs to find him at the bottom of the steps. There he sat with his big brown eyes, afraid to come past the third step because it creaked. "It's okay, Win. It's just a little noise. You can do it," I told him over and over.

He looked at me as if to say, "No, I can't do it. I'm really scared." His big face looked so worried.

I found some leftover steak from dinner to lure him up the steps. That didn't work. Next, I tried a chunk of his favorite cheddar cheese. That didn't work. That always works with him for anything! At that point, I was freezing in the kitchen, searching the fridge for a miracle treat. He waited patiently at the steps.

Finally, one paw at a time, front leg, back leg, I helped him, step-by-step while he trembled with fear. Even at that time of the morning you had to love him. I could feel the weight of his massive body against mine, shaking. Nothing I said soothed him. We slowly made it to the fourth step of safety, and then he sprinted up the stairs.

At night, his favorite place to sleep was on my pillow. That was not my husband's favorite place for him to be! In fact, Scott never let him up on the bed. But after that stressful experience with the evil, creaking step, I felt so bad for him I didn't tell him to get down.

I could feel him slowly move one paw onto the bed. The mattress dipped a little. Then another leg came up. Again, the mattress dipped. Finally I could feel his huge body slowly, gently climb onto the bed. He'd made it! Dad was still asleep. He'd completed his stealth move! He quickly closed his eyes and let out a huge sigh of relief. I didn't have the heart to push him off. As I put my arm over him, he fell fast asleep and began to snore.

When our cat had four kittens in the hall closet, we worried that Winston might hurt them. We moved Mama and babies upstairs into my daughter's room. Jamie had removed her door and replaced it with hanging beads. Winston was petrified of those beads. Sometimes he would stop halfway down the hall and lie down. He would not go within ten feet of them.

When the kittens were a few weeks old, we invited Winston into Jamie's room to meet the kitties. First we had to coax him past those treacherous beads. That took ten minutes.

There he stood, towering over the box, staring at the four black and white kittens nuzzling their mom. He whimpered and stared, still shaking with excitement.

I imagined he was thinking, "Mom, what did you bring home now? Are they my brothers and sisters? I hope they stay in that box." As they grew older, they'd chase his tail and climb all over him. He was a gentle giant.

We usually came home right after work every night, but one night we decided to stop off for take-out seafood. When we got home, Winston was not himself. His belly looked swollen, and he kept nudging my husband. It was seven o'clock when I called our vet.

Could she see him tonight? She'd have to get a babysitter and call me back.

Ten minutes later, I called again in a panic. "I think he's dying," I cried into the phone.

"Bring him right in," she told us.

Before we could get him to the truck, he passed away on our kitchen floor. I sat holding his head, telling him he was such a good boy. Our family cried for days. Our kids' friends rushed over to say goodbye to him.

I wish we'd known about the seriousness of this condition called bloat. Winston was seven when he died. He was healthy and active, and I think he could have lived many more years, had we known it requires emergency surgery. We haven't gone out for seafood since.

We have a picture of Winston, with his big head and paws, hanging out of our front screen door. He broke so many screens trying to see who was coming to visit that we finally gave up and just let him look out the door.

The Dog Whisperer would be horrified!

Every time I look at that photo, I say, "Awww, Winston, you were such a good boy."

And then I cry.

Purple Cow

During seventh grade, I came home to find my gran serving tea to six nuns in our kitchen. My teacher, Sister Mary Theresa, was one of them. She was ironing our clothes. Seriously, my teacher was ironing my uniform blouse.

"Hello, Anne!" she said, "Come sit with us for a cup of tea." Apparently, she had offered to iron while Gran searched for scones. I still wasn't sure how they arrived until my dad appeared with a wrench in his hand.

"Jimmy, you are a blessing," one of the nuns said in her Irish accent.

He just smiled. "I almost have the radiator fixed. By the time you're done with your tea, I'll have you back on the road."

"How can we ever repay you for this kind gesture?"

My dad thought for a minute. "Well, if you ever decide to sell that wagon, I'd be interested."

I looked at him and thought, "What is he going to do with the nuns' station wagon?"

Years passed and the nuns came by one day. They had vowed to keep their promise. Their station wagon was up for sale.

My dad was thrilled, and I wondered who was going to drive that thing. It was a beast of heavy metal. My dad loved it, but I thought it was the ugliest thing I'd ever seen.

My friend picked me up for high school in a brand new pale blue Malibu convertible. It had a white interior, a pinstripe, and her initials on the door. When something was wrong with that car, she drove her dad's Mercedes. I was used to riding in style.

Much to my chagrin, guess what I drove? You guessed it! The nuns' wagon. The Blessed Mother statue was glued to the dashboard with something they must use at NASA. She would not come off; she just rocked and rolled along with the bumps.

Under the streetlights at night, the car turned to a deep purple color. I christened her the Purple Cow. I thought this beast was hideous to begin with but at night it was horrible. My friend's Malibu was the same color, day or night.

Friday night came and we had plans to go to a dance. I was the only one who could drive, so I sadly picked my friends up in my Purple Cow. By now, the floor on the shotgun side had developed a hole. When I drove through a puddle, the person in that seat had to pull their legs up really fast, or they'd get soaked. There was a lot of screaming when that happened. I parked far away from the dance so no one would see the Purple Cow.

Once I'd driven it to work, and when I came out … it was gone! Someone had stolen my Purple Cow! I called my dad and he met me with the police to take a report. The next morning, the police called to say they had found it.

"Come on, Anne," Dad said. "Let's go bring her home."

When we arrived, the officer was waiting at the car. "This is a sturdy piece of wheels you have here, Mr. Lawless." My dad smiled, appreciating the compliment. "When we catch him, we'll call you to see if you want to press charges."

A week later, we learned that a teenage boy had taken it for a joy ride and just left it in a parking lot. Years later, my brother-in-law met my dad for the first time. "You look so familiar," he said, rubbing his face trying to place him.

Guess who he was ... the Purple Cow thief!

We had two-hour rides to the Jersey shore every summer in that wagon. Seven of us were crammed in the car with suitcases on top, a dog in the back with my grandmother, and enough food to last a year.

Did I mention that the Purple Cow didn't have air conditioning? The only person getting any air was sitting shotgun where the growing hole in the floor created a little breeze. Between the sweaty bodies, the dog drooling, Gran snoring, and my dad singing country-western songs, it felt like a six-hour drive.

Back then, I felt so embarrassed by that car. Now, I'd give anything to take that drive one more time—on a sunny day, of course.

The Hottie Test

really thought I'd lost it. I didn't feel hot anymore. I don't mean hot flashes, I mean hot, like a sexy lady … a Hottie. I used to be hot. In my twenties men would ask me to date them or just go to their apartment. After I had five children, and now three grandkids, they stopped calling. My husband kept hanging up on them!

I decided it was time to pass my old Hottie crown to the younger babes. This was not a happy moment for me. Although I've tried to lose my baby weight, it has not gone as well as I'd hoped. My youngest is thirty-one and if I'd lost a pound for each birthday, I'd still have my crown. Alas, that is not the case.

It's not just the menopausal pouch. It's a combination of elephant ear arms, a wrinkle-a-day arrival and, memory loss. Even if I was a Hottie, I'd probably forget and wear my granny panties daily. I was going to start a novena to the Patron Saint of Menopause, but I couldn't remember his name … or her name. Somebody up there knows. And then it happened!

A miracle! My prayers were answered. The very next morning, I realized that I still have it! I grabbed my Hottie crown back so fast I almost got dizzy. What a relief to feel like my sexy self again. I knew somewhere deep down I still had it. Maybe you are like me and also wondering if you still have it. I'll share my test with you.

Step 1: Get a five-pound bag of miniature chocolate bars. They call it an industrial size.

Step 2: Put on your favorite lingerie, no granny panties for this test. Prop yourself up in bed and get comfy. Fluff your pillows and prepare.

Step 3: Remove six bars from the bag and eat five. Peel the wrapper off the chocolate. Try not to lick the wrapper, please. That looks so unsexy and it defeats our purpose. Delicately place the first bar between your lips. Savor the chocolate as it melts slowly in your mouth. Do not chomp. Savor. Continue until you have finished all five bars.

Step 4: Place the last bar under the covers.

Step 5: Go to sleep and dream about how beautifully sexy you are. Do not, under any circumstances, search for that bar under the covers. You will contaminate the test area.

Step 6: In the morning, wake slowly. There is no rush. Stretch, yawn, and stretch some more. Go to the bathroom, brush your teeth, and wipe the sleepy winks from your eyes.

Step 7: Gently lift the comforter from your bed and search for the last chocolate bar. When you find it, gently scoop it up and feel the texture. Do not be tempted to eat the chocolate. If the packet feels soft and warm with a liquid texture, you have passed the Hottie Test.

Note: It is always best to do this test several times. A false/positive result can occur.

I've eaten fifteen pounds of chocolate bars proving my theory. I didn't want to announce to the world that I am still a Hottie until I had confirmed all of the evidence. And now

I can proclaim to the world that for the past ninety nights, I have endured intense physical testing and I have passed. Let me introduce myself: Anne Bardsley, the sixty-one-year-old Hottie with chocolate on her face!

Disney Trip

For an entire year, we planned our vacation to sunny Florida. The biggest highlight for the kids was the amusement parks. My husband was questioning the twenty-four hour drive in our old Suburban van. As luck would have it, we passed a car dealership within a half hour. He almost gave us whiplash as he turned into the lot.

Ten minutes later, we were testing a brand new, dark blue conversion van. And my husband calls me impulsive! Seriously, who does that? Within minutes after the test drive, he signed the papers, and we were the proud owners of a shiny new van. It was complete with a TV/VCR, captain's chairs, reclining seats, and a pull-out bed in the last row. It was fabulous!

Finally, we were speeding down the highway in our new, classy van. We looked like royalty in the captain's chairs. The kids were reclined in the back watching TV. This was heaven! Nirvana, even!

Four hours into the trip, the honeymoon was over. Everyone was starving. Nobody liked the same channel. Erika complained that Jamie was crunching chips too loudly. Jamie disagreed and made her opinion known with her mouth full of chips. Someone stunk. Justin complained that Tom kept looking at him. Tom yelled that everyone should just, "Shut up!"

Then I heard Justin say, "Mom, make him stop looking at me!"

"You are really ugly! Did Mom and Dad ever tell you that?" Tom asked Justin.

I am not proud of my behavior, but I screamed like a lunatic, "No one looks very beautiful to me at this moment in time. Stop looking and crunching and, for God's sake, who smells? If this keeps up, Dad and I will hitch a ride at the next rest stop. I hope you all have a happy life!" Complete silence followed for the next sixty miles.

Bright and early the next morning, we were ready for fun and adventure. That's when the real trouble started. Tom jumped out of the van first and stormed off because the girls had been teasing him. He had been cooped up far too long, and they were far too close. By the time we got the rest of our gang together, Tom was nowhere in sight. We had lost him!

I was in a panic! He was twelve years old and the park was huge. Scott, on the other hand, calmly said, "He can't go anywhere without us. He can't drive. They'll probably page us to come get him." Back in the 1980s life was simpler and safer, but just the same, I felt crazed with worry.

After we scoured the huge parking lot and couldn't find him, we headed into the park. I was a mess! I prayed to Saint Anthony to find him. I sprained my neck muscles from twisting left, then right, searching for him.

"Scott, what if we don't find him?"

"Oh, he'll show up. Enjoy the park."

Three hours went by and suddenly who should come walking down the main street but Tom, with a big smile on his face. "Hey, they let me in and fed me all this food. I love this place!"

By then, I wanted to hug him and choke him. "Stay with us," I said, "so you don't get lost again, please." I looked away for a moment and when I looked back, he was off in another direction. This time, I decided that Scott was right. Tom would find us again.

We stayed a little longer than planned. When we got back that night, there was smoke and an odd smell coming from our rental condo. I had forgotten that I put a turkey in the oven on 200-degrees before we left that morning. The smoke alarms were going off, and the turkey looked like a smoking black bowling ball. There was a fire truck coming down the road.

I didn't remember seeing this vision in the brochures. There were princesses, and castles, and magic slippers, promising me a week of pure escape and delight. There was no smoke billowing out of a condo in the pictures. The families walked hand in hand together through the parks and they were smiling! It promised the best family vacation ever!

After the smoke was gone, I asked the biggest fireman where I could get a pair of ruby slippers. I was ready to click three times and go home.

Mr. Bojangles

June 18, 1967 started out like any other Saturday morning. My alarm buzzed twice, but I was still in bed. Herman's Hermits were singing my favorite song on the clock radio, "Something tells me I'm into something good."

My mother's shrill voice interrupted my dream of Herman. "Get out of bed. Now! Candy stripers are important volunteers. You can't be late on your first day."

Then the usual warnings, "Don't talk to strangers. Be careful. Make sure you get bus number 142. Are you sure you don't want me to drive you and Mariah?"

"Mom, no!" I protested. "We want to take the bus."

Mariah was waiting for me at the corner of our old grade school. We'd be fourteen and freshmen in the fall, so we felt very grown up. There we stood in our freshly starched red-and-white-striped uniforms. Sporting thick-soled shoes, we had more support on our feet than in our bras.

Right on time, old number 142 rattled to our stop. The bus was full, so we made our way to the very back, away from all the old people who were coughing and making disgusting noises.

At the next bus stop an elderly man, looking worn and ragged, struggled up the steps. He banged his suitcase and an old crate against each row of seats. We snickered at the sight of him.

Suddenly, it dawned on me that this could be the stranger my mother had warned me about. My heart pounded in my chest. I was in a state of panic when he sat down right next to me. I froze. Before I could plan my escape, he let out a loud sigh, turned to me, and said, "Good morning," rather pleasantly.

I could barely look at him. He smelled old and his teeth were crooked. His hair hadn't seen shampoo in quite some time. His tan plaid trousers were so worn that small holes dotted his pant leg.

As we reached the next stop, I heard a sharp yelping noise come from the rusty crate. A pair of brown, beady eyes stared at me.

The old man crooned softly to the creature. "Oh, so you want to meet the girls? Come on then." He gingerly lifted out an adorable, and equally ragged, small mutt. He lifted her gently and introduced us to Gracie.

The old stranger had come to life. His blue eyes sparkled and his smile broadened. He handed Gracie to me and her warm body fit in the curve of my arm. She was a rumpled mess of grizzled blonde fur. Her eyes hid behind tufts of slightly matted hair and her little paws were spreading specks of dirt onto my newly starched uniform. He grinned and asked me, "Would you like to dress her?"

Before I could answer, he lifted the suitcase onto his lap. It was brown, blotchy, and covered with faded stickers from Alabama, Tennessee, and Louisiana. Inside, he had it neatly partitioned into two sections.

His part of the suitcase held a few plaid shirts and pants. Gracie, on the other hand, had a complete wardrobe of colorful dresses, bonnets, and bows. I looked from the suitcase and back into his eyes. I heard myself ask, "Can I dress her?"

I chose a frilly pink-and-white dress with layers of worn crinoline underneath. It had a dainty pearl necklace sewn into the collar. Mariah handed me the matching white hat.

Gracie sat ever so still, offering her paws, one at a time, as her thin legs slipped through the armholes. I buttoned the dress very carefully. She didn't even flinch when I tied her bonnet. Her fuzzy ears poked through the slits. She looked gorgeous!

As if on cue, she jumped off my lap and sat at the old man's feet. He was lost in time now, leaning back, legs sprawled, and smiling to himself. This little mutt charmed my friend and me, and the man knew it.

He looked into our eyes and with a twinkling smile, he reached into his ripped pocket and pulled out a weathered harmonica. He put the old harpoon to his lips and, with a wink of his eye, he started the show.

A lively rendition of "Oh Susannah" filled the back of the bus. Gracie was transformed into a showgirl. Ever so gracefully, her fur-balled little body twirled like a ballerina. Her front paws moved in the air as she spun to the music.

By now, everyone in the entire back of the bus was enjoying the show. We all clapped and laughed as they finished their performance. All too soon, our destination, the Bryn Mawr Hospital, came into view. I wanted to stay on the bus and let the show go on but duty was calling.

The old man reached into his pocket and said, "Here's something for your trouble. Buy yourselves a soda."

"Oh, we couldn't take your money, sir. Buy Gracie some bones with it," I said as I waved goodbye and stepped to the curb.

ANNE BARDSLEY

Every day for the rest of that summer, I would look for the two of them to get back on the bus, but they never did. I'm sure by now they are in Heaven. I wonder how many lives they touched on their journey.

For a long time, I felt so guilty; my initial thoughts about him were so unkind. After all these years, the memory of that silly little dog in a dress, and that smiling old man, still warms my soul. I keep them safely tucked away on a shelf in my heart.

Maybe one day, I'll make a similar lasting impression in someone else's life.

The Dry Cleaners

Scott has decided to change up his fashion status. Instead of leisure short-sleeve shirts, he's now wearing oxford-style shirts. I immediately felt a wave of inadequacy overcome me. I had visions of the dryer buzzer going off when I am miles away and those damn shirts wrinkling by the second. This causes me stress. I DO NOT IRON! I don't even own an ironing board (no judgments, please). I have a severe case of "iron-itis." I get hot flashes and I curse when I am forced to iron. My house is a no-iron zone.

He looks very handsome in his pressed shirts. After I reminded him about my condition, he promised to take them to the dry cleaners. And for a few weeks he did. Some weeks he even picked them up. Yesterday he asked me to drop three shirts off for him and pick up his clean ones. I asked, "What kind of starch do you ask for? Light? Medium? Heavy?"

His response was, "Just tell her my name. She knows me." Hmm ... she knows him.

I decided to test his theory. I walked in and a strawberry blonde with curly hair was at the counter. She was very pleasant. She asked my name, and I watched for a response. I thought since she "knows him" she might be surprised to see his wife picking up his laundry. The name did not register with her.

I handed her the three shirts to be cleaned, and she asked how I wanted them done. I mentioned, "He says you'll know. You know him," with a straight face.

I watched her step back, and her eyes searched to the left and then to the right. Her brow furrowed. "What is his name again?" she asked. "No, I don't know him. I'm so sorry, but I have no idea how he likes his shirts." She looked as if she was confessing that she did indeed take those shirts off my husband in a sleazy hotel.

"It's okay," I told her, "just do them like his last batch. He thinks everyone knows him. He thinks he's special." I left the store laughing as I said, "Welcome to my world. It's a good thing he's a good guy or I'd ship him over to you."

She laughed and said, "Oh no! I'm sure he's a good guy. You keep him."

When Scott arrived home he asked how his friend at the dry cleaners was.

"She didn't remember you."

"What? She knows me! We laugh every time I go in there. She thinks I look like Hulk Hogan with my mustache."

Ever since a few old ladies at his dad's nursing home screamed, "The Hulk is in the house," he uses this line. I mentioned that the women are almost one hundred years old and their eyesight might not be the best, but he dismissed me.

"Ah-ha! So that's how she knows you." I grinned watching his reaction to being not so unforgettable. "Does your friend have strawberry blonde curly hair?"

"No, she has black hair."

"That explains everything." The mystery had been solved.

"Well, I feel better now," he said. "She knows how Hulk likes his shirts, I mean … I like my shirts with medium starch on a hanger." A little reality check might be in order here. He might have not only the mustache, but the ego of Hulk as well.

"What's her name?" I asked.

"I don't know her. She just knows me."

I was about to ship him off to the strawberry blonde lady, but he really is a good guy.

We all like to feel special. If all it takes is to have the lady at the dry cleaners know that you like medium starch in your shirts and put on a hanger, that's one simple man. Let those wonderful people wash, starch, and iron on! And don't forget … he's special.

Toned Up and Tuned In

ately, I find my friends to be too intense. Last week I was in the bakery department sampling the deal of the day, cherry cheesecake bites, when they arrived from an exercise class wearing sweaty leotards. Mary confessed that she has an addiction to aerobics. Kelly was addicted to yoga.

I popped a cherry cheesecake bite into my mouth. "Oh, I am so sorry to hear that. There are twelve-step programs everywhere now," I said sincerely. They stared at me like two well-toned deer caught in the headlights of an oncoming Mack truck.

I went on to tell them that I also had workout equipment. "Yes, I'm using my step-board with three extensions." They were extremely impressed. I didn't share that I had raised it higher to hold my laundry basket so I didn't have to keep bending over. They don't need to know everything. I offered them each a piece of Danish. They declined and, as they walked away, I stuffed another cherry cheesecake bite into my mouth.

On my way home, I thought maybe they were right. I should be more in-tune with my body. I attempted to throw the last cherry cheesecake bite out the car window, feeling only slightly guilty that there are starving children in the world. The darn thing fell back onto my lap. I knew it was a sign, so I ate it. I positioned my visor mirror, pushed the crumbs off my legs, and said aloud to no one in particular, "Anne, today you are making a brand new start. Today you get in shape!"

Now three months later, I am still committed to my program. I have a new attitude. I look good. I feel good. James Brown is singing his song "I Feel Good" just for me. Let me share my secret.

Every morning I wake up and the first thing I do is stretch. I do this for five minutes in bed. I try very hard (exercising my mind here, too!) not to doze off.

Once I've stretched, I slowly get out of bed. When my feet touch the floor, I sprint to the coffee pot and flip on the switch. In a matter of minutes, after I sip that first cup, my pulse rate increases. Then I sprint back to bed and continue my stretching under the covers. Sometimes I doze from the exhaustion of the sprint.

Throughout the day, I keep a healthy mindset. At lunch last week with my healthy friends, they had mixed berry yogurt. I had a marvelous strawberry shortcake. The strawberries counted as fruit, therefore giving me my vitamin C, thank you very much. The whipped cream counted as dairy (I had extra. At this age, I want to have strong bones). I was getting that all-important calcium and vitamin D to avoid osteoporosis. I even sprinkled a few almonds for extra protein. The cake was probably low fat. Who could tell with all those strawberries and whipped cream? I'm sure it was.

My husband noticed my new figure. My old clothes were just hanging off my hips. I didn't share my secret shopping trip to buy larger clothes. For just a few hundred dollars, I look so much thinner. It was just too depressing to squeeze into last year's shorts. It's not good for my mental health to lament over such things.

Once I had my new clothing, I noticed my hair needed some attention. I needed something sassy, just like my new shorts.

I insisted that my hairdresser cut my hair with my head tilted backward.

I told her I had neck spasms. I really just hate to feel my double chin when I put my head down. Neck spasms, mental anguish—it's all the same degree of pain in my book.

So you see, it's really simple to get in shape. It's just mind over matter. I haven't started aerobics yet; I'm still monitoring my pulse and, as soon as it slows down, I'll have another cup of coffee to speed it up. Maybe I'll have a little coffeecake with it so I don't endanger my blood sugar level. I'm still stretching in bed as much as I can. After all, I *am* a health nut.

Organization 101

My husband is the organized one in our family. He even folds his underwear, and they're all in one drawer.

He constantly tries to organize our refrigerator. The kids loved when he did that. They'd yell to him, "Dad, does cheese go on the dairy shelf or the protein shelf?"

Next I'd hear, "There's no room on the dairy shelf, so I made room for the eggs with the chicken. It seemed a perfect match."

Scott would shake his head and moan, "No, no, no! Listen up! Dairy is dairy! Eggs are dairy, but they're also protein. Primarily they're dairy, so keep them on that shelf."

Meanwhile, the refrigerator was back to its normal disarray. We just let him focus on "his dairy shelf." Within two days, the dairy shelf held fruit, chocolate bars (cold chocolate bars are my weakness), celery, some other fresh veggies, and cottage cheese. We're sticking with the dairy theme here ... milk chocolate, cottage cheese, and maybe a cow might chew on a stalk of celery.

He organizes all of his passwords and account numbers by logging them into a little brown notebook. This is the same notebook that I'm not permitted to write in, because it must have neat printing and the ink must be black. I personally think a little color would do that book some good, but he has made it perfectly clear that my additions are not welcome, regardless of my artistic abilities.

This brings me to my next problem. How in the world can any normal person be expected to remember all of these passwords?

My husband's passwords are always unique. He'll see a picture of an airplane and use the numbers on the plane, such as NJ260A.

My personal favorite example of an obscure password was when he chose Viper from the movie *Top Gun*. Then he combined the two for a brilliant password of ViperNJ260A.

Now, how am I supposed to know that? I use my children's birthdates, a combination of my bra and shoe size, or the name of my favorite wrinkle cream … normal things.

My husband also uses our address mixed in with my social security number and his favorite number. Seriously, I am in the midst of menopause. I can barely remember his name, let alone his favorite number. I still don't know what it is.

For a while, he ended all the passwords with XXX. I told him that made us look like porn stars. Get the XXX off that screen!

Sometimes he gets extra inventive and uses half of a birthday with his favorite hockey player's number, the month of our anniversary, and a kid's birthdate. We have five kids. It changes when he gets mad at one kid, and he replaces it with another kid's year.

Do you think I can grasp that with my menopausal mind? It's like a Rubik's cube! I'd wear out a debit machine touch pad trying to get the numbers right. I'd be at the register with ice cream melting all over the place, begging, "Please, please just wait one minute more. I almost have it figured out."

This is what happens when an organized mind meets a menopausal mind. My husband thinks all of these different passwords keep his brain fresh. Well, unless I carry around a notebook of password codes the size of a telephone book, I am lost.

It does not help my brain. It scrambles it. I can do that on my own, thank you very much. And I don't need the additional twenty pounds to lug around.

Last week I could not remember one of his famous passwords. I called the credit card company and the nice woman with a southern accent asked, "Darlin', is your husband there?" Now if he was here, I'd just ask him what the password was! I wouldn't be calling.

"I can't give you any information without speaking to him first. He has to verify that he knows you and gives me permission to talk to you."

"I am telling you he knows me. Just this morning he asked me to make him coffee, wash his laundry, and, time permitting, get amorous before he left for work. Now doesn't that sound just like something he would say?" I asked.

"Well, when I talk to him, I can ask him if that's true," she said politely.

"Ma'am," I insisted, "I'm trying to pay a bill right now and I need that security code. How about if I give you answers and you can tell me if they match the questions?"

Before she could reply, I rattled off, "1948, red Camaro convertible, Warminster, Winston, St. John's church, 1975 maroon MG, Moran, Linda Lane, 1980, Mrs. Martin."

"Is that all?" she asked. This lady was tough. I had to burn more brain cells to please her.

"N6892XXX, Viper8921, NovApr0430, Cess76na, XXXpiper 290, Goose0948." I was breathless now, but without approval. I ended up with a late fee.

In an effort to relieve my stress, I suggested to Scott that we make all of the passwords the same. He stressed this was a very bad thing to do, since it makes identity theft easier. If they crack one code, they can get them all.

I understand the reasoning, so I am now in charge of passwords:

E-mail password: computer

Debit card PIN: 1157
(my mom's birthday month and the HGTV channel)

Amazon: BIG WOMAN

Health insurance: hemoglobin (seemed like a natural)

Electric company: zapme
(I'm afraid to get zapped with 220 volts)

Craigslist: needadeal (get it?)

I even made the alarm system the name of our dog. He barks every time a squirrel goes by our house. It made perfect sense. *Who could forget Murphy?* My husband, that's who.

Just Call Me Babe

When we make breakfast on the hospice floor at the Bay Pines VA Hospital, we meet all sorts of people.

Most people think hospice must be a very sad floor, but there is so much humor there between the sadness. I have fond memories of quite a few patients and their families.

One of my favorites is a man who my husband christened "Robert De Niro." The man looked just like him, with his jet-black hair. Our version did admit that he missed a spot on his temple last time he dyed it.

We got so used to calling him Mr. De Niro that I can't even remember his real name, but I will never forget him. He was in his eighties and had just learned that his cancer was stage four. The week before, he'd been living life and had no idea that he was so sick.

Mr. De Niro had the largest fan club of any man I've ever met. Our kitchen was filled with people who came to visit him. His daughter would answer his cell phone as if she was his secretary.

"Dad, it's Jimmy from the hotel."

"Dad, it's the bartender from Kelly's."

"Dad, it's the mailman."

"Dad, it's Joe from Mazzaro's Restaurant."

He had non-stop phone calls from people who'd just received the news.

One morning as I made breakfast for the crowd, I asked his son-in-law what he would like and he asked my name. I told him, "Anne."

It's a very difficult name to remember, you know. He called me Angela, Amy, and Anna. I finally said, "Just call me Babe!" From there on out, I was Babe to the entire crew.

More families came to breakfast that day and, before I knew it, they were all calling me Babe! The new folks had no idea that it wasn't my real name.

"Babe, can I have more bacon?"

"Babe, can I have two eggs over easy light?"

"Babe, do you have half and half?"

"That was a great breakfast. Thanks, Babe!"

Later, as Mr. De Niro got weaker, we'd see the family gather together. I was so impressed that he made such a difference in so many lives.

I decided that this was how I want to live my life. What a great legend he left for his family and friends!

I told his son-in-law that, so he hugged me and said, "Thanks, Babe." I wiped a tear.

After all these years, I'm finally a Babe!

Me, Matt, the Cat, and the Watermelon

One hot summer afternoon I came home to find my son's friend, Matt, sitting on our front porch. I invited him in so he didn't melt in the heat. Justin would be home shortly. I offered him a glass of iced tea. Like a good hostess, I added fresh lemon and a sprig of something green to impress him.

"Mrs. B," he asked, "do you mind if I have a piece of that watermelon in the fridge?"

"Sure, Matt. I'll cut you a piece. I think there must have been a bad spot because someone cut a piece off the top." I got the knife and cut Matt a big slice. It looked so refreshing, he suggested I have a slice, too. In fact, he cut it for me. I was going to call his mom and tell her what a nice young man she'd raised.

We sat and slurped down this delicious watermelon. We both agreed it was the sweetest we've EVER had. Matt suggested we have another piece while he waited for Justin. I agreed. I was starting to chill from a hectic day and this watermelon was just what I needed to unwind. Matt offered to get up and cut it for me. What a nice kid!

I told Matt he would be a great waiter for a summer job.

"Thanks, Mrs. B, and you don't have to leave me a tip!" he chuckled.

Our cat, appropriately named Kitty, started to scratch at my legs for a treat. I gave her a small piece of the melon. She rolled over and played with it like catnip.

By now, Matt and I were discussing life. "How's your girlfriend?"

"Did you hear what happened to Jill? She cheated on Marty."

"Oh no! That tramp!" I yelled. I wasn't sure where that came from because I actually like Jill.

"I'm not sure she's a tramp, Mrs. B," Matt defended her.

"Oh! You are so naïve, Matt! Matt, sometimes pretty girls can be tramps. It's deceiving because you expect tramps to have cigarettes hanging out of their mouths and their hair all teased up."

I told Matt he was very naïve again. I think I said it three more times. I liked the way it rolled off my tongue.

"Matt, let's have one more piece of melon before Justin gets home. Give Kitty that little piece on your plate. She loves this stuff."

A half hour later, Justin arrived home. Matt, the cat, and I had eaten half of the watermelon.

"Hey Justin, want some watermelon before your mom eats it all?" Matt asked

"Hey! I yelled. Lighten up! It's a fruit! It's healthy! It's a bleeping fruit!"

Justin gave Matt a dirty look and said, "You know what's in the melon, right?"

I said, "Of course, seeds! We're spitting them out." I spit one his way.

I suggested Justin help us finish off this incredibly refreshing and delicious melon quickly because I was feeling very sleepy. Kitty was, too. She fell asleep sitting up at my feet.

When my daughters arrived home they were angry that the watermelon was almost gone. Since when did my kids like fruit so much?

"Who ate the watermelon?" they demanded.

I grinned and announced, "Matt, the cat, and I did." I grinned at them and hiccupped. "It was delishioushhh. Have shome. It's verrrrry nutrishish for you. Watch for the sheeds. Justin says they're in there. Ooops, here comes one now!" I spit it in their direction and laughed uncontrollably. I was having so much fun chilling with my kids, Matt, and the cat.

Scott arrived home to find me and the cat sound asleep on the couch.

"Have you been drinking?" he asked. He stared at me as I tried to upright myself.

"No! I had watermelon with Matt and the cat. Don't be shilly!"

Justin and Matt arrived to confess that the watermelon was the cause of my exhaustion. Matt took the blame. That's when I learned that the hole in the watermelon was not a bad spot. It was a hole to pour vodka into in my refreshing, delicious watermelon. Kitty hiccupped.

Now who's naïve?

Penguin Petting

One Christmas, we had a visit in Florida from my good friend, Betsy, her husband, Tom, and their two sons.

One of the exciting trips she planned for them was to one of the sea mammal theme parks in the area. Their youngest son, Matt, collected penguins. He also had a fear of flying.

In an effort to lure him onto the plane, Betsy booked a special treat: penguin petting.

Matt's older brother, Josh, was not so excited about this very special event, which would happen on a Sunday morning at ten o'clock sharp. Oh, did I mention this was also the day of the Dallas Cowboys and Philadelphia Eagles playoff game?

Betsy's husband is not only an Eagles fanatic, he's also a bodybuilder. Every morning at five o'clock he heads to the gym. He is built like an oak tree. His chest is so large he wears a triple XL shirt and has a thirty-six-inch waist. He can be a little high strung.

We were having a barbecue to celebrate their arrival, and that's when Tom realized that he would be missing the Eagles playing their archrival, the Dallas Cowboys. "Betsy, why didn't you book the penguins on Monday? Or Tuesday? Do you realize what you've done?"

She twirled her naturally curly hair and asked calmly, "Don't you remember our family vacation meeting? Everyone was silent. So I took charge."

This conversation went on and on throughout the night. Every time the thought crossed Tom's mind, he'd start up again. He'd say to my husband, "Hey, Scott, do you want to watch the game tomorrow? Oh, that's right. I can't. Betsy took charge. I'll be penguin petting."

Betsy twirled another section of hair.

Later he said, "Hey, Scott, can we go see the Philly's spring training camp? Oh, that's right, Betsy took charge. I'll be at the theme park."

More hair twirling.

Then he asked, "Hey, Scott, maybe we can take the boys out deep sea fishing before the game starts. Oh, that's right. I'll be driving an hour and a half to pet the penguins because Betsy is still in charge."

After each of these statements, my friend just smiled and said, "That's right. At next year's vacation meeting, speak up!" and continued to twirl her hair.

I was feeling very nervous at that point, because I was afraid she'd have twirled every piece of hair off her head before they made it to the park. Unlike Betsy, I inherited rubbing my chin when I'm stressed.

So the next day, at about half past noon, the phone rang. It was Tom telling us that not only was he missing the football game, but also he was also "Encountering the damn penguin's stink! And there are hundreds of them!"

Matt was in his glory petting the little buggers, and Tom and Josh were heading for the exit in an attempt to escape this entire adventure. They were adjusting their radios, trying to get good reception of the game. Meanwhile, Betsy was snapping pictures as Matt posed with a little creature.

My husband was laughing hysterically, and I was feeling a tad stressed about the whole thing. I rubbed my chin.

An hour went by and the phone rang again. There was penguin poop all over and guess who stepped in it with his new sandals? That's right, old twinkle-toes, Tom!

My husband had a coughing fit from laughing so hard, so I was stuck on the phone as Tom told me the disgusting realities of penguins. I asked if he actually pet one and he said, "Pet one? Anne, I'm standing in penguin poop and it's all over my new sandals. I don't want to go near one!"

I tried to assure him that they were adorable little creatures. "Didn't you see that movie *The March of the Penguins*? Have a heart."

He snarled, "Put Scott back on the phone."

My husband grabbed the phone and smacked my hand away from my chin. Scott started screaming, "He–could–go–all–the–way! Touchdown! Eagles have scored and it's a fourteen to nothing game!" Tom hung up.

Twenty minutes went by and sure enough, the phone rang again.

My husband raced to get the phone first. "Yeah, Tom, I'm here for you. The score is twenty-eight to zero." He then recounted the plays. I could hear Tom groaning. I imagined his bulging eyes, purple face, and his triceps in spasms. My husband said, "I have to go, Tom, the game is back on. I'll call you if they score again. By the way … another touchdown! Oh! You are missing a great game!"

By now, my chin was feeling a little raw, and I went looking for Neosporin. I texted Betsy and she texted back that they were having a wonderful time.

Can't she hear Tom complaining? Maybe they sell earplugs and little dolphin-shaped tablets for stress relief at the gift shop.

I asked how Tom and Josh liked the penguins, and she texted back that Tom had a problem with his sandal and she hasn't seen him. She was just getting ready to have them paged over the intercom when she got my text.

Ten minutes later, the phone rang again. It was Tom. "Scott, it's not bad enough that I got dragged here to pet the penguins, stepped in their mess, and missed the game, but Betsy wants to make this an annual tradition."

My husband was laughing so hard he could barely breathe. I was frantically searching the yellow pages for a plastic surgeon because I have now completely rubbed off my chin!

The Car Wash

t was a lovely morning. I planned to meet an interior decorator downtown at noon sharp. As I went out the door, Scott asked me to get the truck washed after filling it with gas.

"Sure," I said, "a simple run through the car wash is no problem." After I filled the tank, I rushed off to the car wash tunnel. Everyone in front of me was punching numbers into a keypad. They were also holding white receipts. Uh-oh. I didn't have a receipt.

I went back into the convenience store to explain my dilemma to the cashier. There were four people in line in front of me.

The first person could not decide which brand of cigarettes had the least nicotine. The second person only had large bills and argued with the cashier about getting too many small bills in return for change. It was now 11:15 AM and I was tapping my foot.

The next customer, an older woman, bless her heart, didn't speak English. She motioned that she wanted something behind the counter. The cashier couldn't figure out what she meant and they were playing charades. By 11:30 AM, I was ready to jump over the counter and give her anything she wanted for free.

The fourth person only wanted to pay for a soda, thank goodness. I eagerly explained my dilemma and checked my watch once again. I had thirty minutes to make a forty-five minute drive. The cashier said, "Dear, you were in too much of a rush to wait for the printed receipt with the car wash code on it."

"Thank you, dear," I snarled politely.

New code in hand, I pushed my mirrors in, got back in the truck, and waited in line for the car wash.

The light flashed green for me to proceed. As this was happening, I had a dreaded feeling in my stomach. I ignored it.

Something akin to the spray of a dribbling elephant splashed the front of my car and that was all. Nothing else happened. Since this was my virgin trip, I assumed that I should accelerate and proceed through the huge metal arms with still hanging brushes.

So I inched up, a little at a time until the flashing red signs lit up, warning me to, "BACK UP. BACK UP. BACK UP." I did and I waited for something to happen.

Nothing happened, so I proceeded again, trying to activate this beast of steel. There I sat in the tunnel going forward and reverse for ten minutes.

Finally, I found the paper with the code number and called the store. "I am stuck in your car wash," I told the woman.

"Oh dear! That's never happened before," she told me.

"Well, it's happening now. What should I do?"

"Come back to the store, and I'll get you a new code." We hung up and I drove at Andretti speed, frustrated. The woman handed me a new code and a free air freshener to lighten my mood. "Good luck," she said sweetly.

I headed back to the line, which was now three cars deep. They were all just gliding through the brushes with ease.

ANNE BARDSLEY

No BACK UP lights flashing at them.

Just then, my husband called. "How's it going?" he asked.

"Well, I just got stuck in the car wash. It's not good. I'm never getting a vehicle washed again."

"How could you get stuck?" he asked, chuckling. He thought I was kidding.

My blood pressure was rising as I explained. "Did you know you need a receipt with a code on it?"

"Of course! It's printed on the gas receipt. Everyone knows that."

"No, I didn't get a receipt."

"You probably pulled away too fast. Always in a hurry," he counseled me.

That was when I backed out of the car wash and drove off in a dirty truck. Who would think it would be such an ordeal?

I was there for thirty minutes! My nerves were shot. I canceled my appointment. I had to go to a drive-thru restaurant and get a quarter-pound cheeseburger, fries, and a Diet Coke to get a carbohydrate calm.

The saying goes that when you look good, you feel good.

It's not the same with my truck. When my truck looks good, I'm very stressed!

Sweet Crunches

My husband stopped our membership at the gym. He decided that if we put a treadmill, weights, and a bike in our guest room, we would have our own personal in-house gym. We'll be able to work out every day at our convenience.

The funny thing is, he actually believes that I will use this equipment. God love him! He is ever the optimist!

When we belonged to the gym, everyone knew him when he checked in. When I checked in, they treated me like a total stranger. I found this very unfriendly. Whatever happened to southern hospitality?

I'm sure I went at least eight times in the past six months. I was the one who requested White Zinfandel at the yogurt bar. Am I so unforgettable?

I know some women who love to work out, but I am not so inclined. I'm actually more the reclined type. My husband is absolutely mystified that I don't share his love for exercise.

He loves to sweat. Says it makes him feel alive. At sixty-four, he still loves the gym. He trots on the treadmill every day. His sneakers squeak on the rubber tread. He is so busy singing along with his MP3 player, he has no idea that he squeaks. Sometimes, he holds an imaginary microphone and sings aloud to Metallica's "Sandman." And that's when I head for the yogurt bar.

I just don't feel so inspired while sweating. I start getting woozy after just turning the treadmill on. When that happens I know I need to dash for the automated ice cream machine to bring my blood sugar levels back up.

Note that I am very concerned about my health. The ice cream also prevents osteoporosis, so it's a double blessing. I think that the toffee-nut crunch fudge bar works best.

I always ask people how they've lost weight, but I'm not thrilled with their answers.

"Cut down on sweets, exercise, and drink more water."

Boring! I'm holding out for a chocolate-covered pill that will do it all. It would be even better if it whitened my teeth, thickened my hair, and firmed my thighs.

Just last night, I had a dream that there's a new guaranteed weight loss peach cobbler martini! I'm breaking into a sweat just thinking about the possibilities.

Years ago, in my youth, I was so thin that my hipbones actually stuck out. I looked like a commercial for hip replacement, but I thought it was a great look.

Now I can't even find those bones. I think they're well-disguised by my anti-osteoporosis remedy. I tried to poke in there and find them, but I must be doing a really good job with that toffee-nut crunch.

Great news, though—I have the strongest bones on earth!

Scott would be very proud of my crunches. It would break his heart if he knew I was actually crunching my toffee-nut fudge bar instead of my stomach muscles.

Since summer is just a few months away, I'm thinking I should try this workout thing again.

I'll need a fridge for my sugar fix.

Naturally, I'll need new clothes and a shorter haircut.

Oh, and more good news … the treadmill has a built-in fan. I'll look like a model with my hair blowing in the wind.

I just hope it doesn't melt my toffee-nut crunch fudge bar too fast!

Fluff and Stuff

The subject was bound to come up sooner or later. When we die, what do we want done with our remains?

My husband decided he would prefer a cremation. I should get a nice urn and have his ashes sprinkled over water. I should rent a small plane and when the pilot is low and slow over the Gulf of Mexico, I should release his ashes.

The problem I have with that plan is that when Scott used to take me flying, I was not the best passenger. He loved to take steep turns as I held on, leaning in the opposite direction in pure fear. I actually believed that if I leaned far enough, I could somehow level out the plane. It never worked.

He also loved aerobatic flying. I was so grateful that the Pitts Special aerobatic plane was never mentioned for his release. The thought no sooner entered my mind and I heard him say, "I think I'd prefer being in a Pitts Special doing a tailslide."

Once we had his plan established and I stopped crying, he asked, "What shall I do with you?" His eyes looked sad. Neither of us enjoyed talking about these plans of our demise.

"I'd prefer to be stuffed," I told him as I blew my nose.

He shook his head, "What did you say?"

I repeated, "I want to be stuffed. I want you to find a taxidermist who will make me look marvelous. I'm hoping they'll have some sort of gel so you can pose me."

"Why in God's name would I want to pose you? You'll be dead!"

This man is totally clueless! "If I die first and you bring women home, I want to be looking like serious competition in the bedroom. You know that Lifestyle Lift I want? Get me one with my insurance money. I'm hoping that by the time I die, there will be scientific methods to keep me limber. I could be like a female Gumby."

He put his head in his hands.

"Seriously, you could move me from room to room. Since I'll just have new stuffing, I won't be heavy. If you're sitting on the deck, just bring me out. Put a glass of wine in front of me and party on!"

I was feeling much better now. Death didn't seem so final and sad. I could still light up his life, so to speak, like a dim bulb.

Scott mentioned this idea to my brother-in-law and he suggested having a bag made to fit over my head so women think I'm just a clotheshorse.

"Now that is just disrespectful!" I growled.

The more I think of this plan, the more ideas I come up with. He could dress me to match the seasons and holidays. Since I'd be pliable, it would be easy to change my outfits. I could even be a decoration on our front porch. I could be Mrs. Claus at Christmas and a witch at Halloween. The possibilities are endless!

He always wondered what I'd look like with brown eyes. This would be his big chance. He could purchase removable eyes on Amazon and a few wigs, and I could be the woman of his dreams. The after- world is looking pretty bright.

Scott is calling me to go have a glass of wine with him on the deck now. I wonder if I should wait to see if he comes to carry me out. He's going to need the practice!

Professional Mourner

My sister Pat is two years younger than me. We were very different growing up. She was a tomboy and athletic. I was not. She was a cheerleader who could do flips and splits without screaming. I could not.

When she got mad at me, she would cut the hair off my dolls. Since she didn't play with dolls, I had no way to retaliate.

When I was about thirteen, we used to play with a few friends in our basement. We liked to pretend that we were the Beatles. I was John. Pat was Ringo. Our friends were Paul and George.

Once I jumped up with my tennis racquet guitar at the end of a song, and smashed my head on the low ceiling. This sent Pat into fits of laughter. She could do it with ease. She was also a few inches shorter than me.

I couldn't sing, but Pat could. She joined the choir at our grade school, St. Katherine's Elementary. They sang at Mass and funerals.

One day, my mom got a call that there was a problem with Pat in the choir. I heard her say, "Yes, she does have a beautiful voice. She does what?" That caught my attention. What did she do? Nothing brought me more pleasure than knowing Pat was in trouble.

The choir director told Mom that she thought Pat should quit the choir. Apparently, she was crying louder at funerals than the families of the lost loved one. When the organ music stopped, the whole church could still hear Pat bawling in the loft.

Pat took the news hard. She refused to quit! She said she would work on her crying fits. We all waited for the next funeral.

Two weeks later, another funeral was scheduled. This was her big moment to prove herself. The first song, "On Eagles Wings," went fine. The second song was "Let There Be Peace on Earth," and she got teary. By the third song, "Ave Maria," Pat was in full emotional distress.

The family of the deceased actually comforted her after the funeral.

"Oh, sweetheart," a woman with red eyes said, "I didn't know you knew Joseph. You must have loved him very much."

My sister blew her nose and asked, "Who is Joseph?"

She quit the choir.

The Letter of Recommendation

My friend, Betsy, asked me to write a letter of recommendation for my like-a-nephew, Josh, for college. Josh has taken honor courses since he was five. He is very smart and we are all in awe of his brains. His mom even looked at an online genealogy website to see how this happened. She's still looking, but confident someone with brains will show up soon. I had to get this letter out. The due date was approaching and so I wrote the following:

Dear Honor Society,

I have no idea why my good friend asked me to write this letter for her son, Josh. All the kid wants to do is sleep. I hope you can wake him up for classes. Yes, he is a wonderful and smart kid. He came from my friend's loins, so that's to be expected! Let me just tell you that they have GREAT genes in their family. Not only are they flexible (and I mean flexible) in what life throws their way, they can also adapt to almost any situation quickly. You'll notice that with Josh when you teach him all that chemistry and schemistry. I can't seem to remember those classes since I graduated in 1970 ... but I look much younger. Some people are blessed with eternal youth.

I'm a firm believer in emotional IQ. None of those brains matter if you can't decide what kind of Blizzard you want at

Dairy Queen. Did I mention that my friend used to work at a Dairy Queen in her chubby years? She was no slacker like her dozing son, Josh. If we could wake him, I think he'd order a chocolate twisty cone with sprinkles, but we'll never know, will we? The kid is a sleep machine! But I know you'll just love him. He seems to learn as he sleeps. He is truly a dream student. He's amazing and very cooperative. If he ever wakes up and actually speaks, you'll notice he has a very deep voice. I think he has a future in broadcasting. He also has beautiful blue eyes, or are they brown? If he opens them again I'll let you know. He is quite tall. In fact, he is exactly the size of the sofa he sleeps on all day.

The girls at the university will also love him. Who wouldn't love a boyfriend who never disagrees with you? There was that slight issue at the junior prom when he slept through pictures. What kind of date would let them take that picture with his drool all over her shoulder? Seriously! He looked like the guy from *Weekend at Bernie's*. I told him to dump her. I hope he heard me. I just know he would have had so much fun if he'd been able to stay awake.

If you need more information about my like-a-nephew, please ask my husband. He just loves Josh, and I know he'll have many accolades. I'd ask him myself, but he's sleeping too.

One last thing I should mention. Josh doesn't do that volunteer stuff. He is too busy trying to squeeze a dollar out of his neighbors with those ugly dogs he watches. The sound of folding dollars does seem to wake him up. So if you really want him to join your fancy-schmancy society, I think you'll have a real winner. I don't want to say anymore and give him a big head, so I'll sign off now.

Sincerely,

Josh's eternally young like-an-aunt from Florida

(who resembles a beauty queen ... only different ... very different)

Pillow Talk

At three in the morning I heard my husband wake up to go to the bathroom. When he came back to bed, I could feel his usual flipping of the covers, and he sighed deeply.

Then I heard him say, "Do you think I should cut my hair?" He was silent for a few minutes. Then another deep sigh. "I am so tired lately. Maybe it's my thyroid." Silence … sigh.

"I really should join that gym." Silence. Another sigh.

I giggled under the covers and told him to stop.

"Have you noticed that my teeth are getting whiter?" Sigh. "I only ask that to see if my whitening strips are working."

"Why did I eat those potato chips?" he continued. Silence … sigh. "Do you think my legs are getting fatter?"

"Now stop!" I told him.

"I really think I'm getting chubby."

Why was I listening to him at this time of the morning anyway?

"I really have to get my hair cut." Silence … sigh.

"So you agree I need a haircut? How about a new color too?"

he asked. This piqued my interest. I am never too tired to talk about my hair.

"My nails are a mess. French manicure or pink and white?" Silence … sigh.

I started to drift off, but then he started again.

"Oh, these hormones! Maybe I should stop taking them." Silence and two big sighs.

Okay, so I do say that one a lot.

"I need a nap." He yawned.

I was starting to feel sleepy and yawned too.

"Maybe I should leave my hair long." Silence, and a sigh. "Oh, I need more wrinkle cream." Silence … big sigh.

"Thanks for reminding me," I told him and smacked him.

"Does my face look old?" Silence … sigh.

I put the pillow over my head.

"Maybe I should do Zumba." He was silent for a long time … two sighs. "I am just so confused lately!" Silence … loud sigh.

It sounded like he was winding down. By four o'clock, he had covered every possible thing I've ever said.

Who knew he was listening?

One Hot Mess

My hot flashes are almost over. My husband only refers to sleeping with an oven a few times a week.

It wasn't so bad when we lived up north in the cold. In Florida, our bedroom turns into the tropics when I heat up. He says I actually burn him at night. I think he might be exaggerating, but even the dogs sleep on his side of the bed.

Once, we all got tangled up in the covers and I was like a mummy in the morning. Husband on one side, two dogs on the other, I thought for sure I'd shrivel up and die from dehydration before breakfast.

Sleep is not a problem. My new bio-identical hormones are starting to congregate in my cells. My biggest challenge in this almost post-menopausal time is the inability to concentrate. In fact, I can barely remember to take those lovely little hormones daily.

In addition to being forgetful, I'm also living with a very fast-paced brain in my little slow-paced body. To be honest, it's not that little. I'm trusting that the hormones will correct that soon too.

I'm also hoping they will whiten my teeth, erase my wrinkles, tone my thighs, and sprout a money tree in my back pocket. *See what I mean?* Here I am explaining my forgetfulness, and my mind has jumped to a money tree in my pocket!

Just last week, I went shopping for a new bathing suit. I found the perfect halter-topped black suit, which could double as a sundress. It flowed over my hips, and I didn't even have to hold my stomach in. What a great find!

When I got home, I modeled my new suit for my husband. I twirled around the family room so he could see how it flowed. This was possibly the best bathing suit of my entire life! I even put on sandals and hoop earrings to show him the sundress look. He agreed. "Wow! That suit makes you look like you're thirty!"

It wasn't until I went back in and put it in my closet that I noticed the tag, "Maternity by the Bay." Argh! I'd purchased a maternity bathing suit! Worse yet, it fit!

Now being the optimist that I am, I found I could wear this beauty. In fact, as I was walking to the beach, I could feel that pouch that an eight-month pregnant woman would fill out naturally. It felt like an empty nest for my uterus.

I realized that I could probably fill that pouch with suntan lotion, my Kindle, a beach towel, and very possibly two small beach chairs. I might even have room for a cold beverage, but not too chilled. I am now a sunbathing kangaroo! I can wear that suit and I can laugh about it now.

The mix-up did get my attention though. I realized it was time to slow down. My husband says I need to reduce my mental speed from 125 mph to 25 mph. At least that's what I think he said. He talks way too slow for me, and I was making mental notes for things I had to do that day. I just agreed with him and said, "That makes perfect sense. I'll definitely slow down."

The very next morning, I had decaf coffee to start me in my new slow mode.

I went for my annual physical. While the nurse entered my blood pressure on my chart, she asked my age.

I had to think for a minute, reducing my mental mph, and told her, "I am thirty-six or thirty-eight, depending." I smiled at her. I was very proud that my mind was in slow-mo.

She gave me blank stare and asked, "Well, which is it? Are you thirty-seven?"

I was a bit confused by that question, so I repeated my answer. "No! I am thirty-six or thirty-eight, depending."

"Depending on what?" She was barking at me now. I was about to explain to her that different manufacturers have different fits. That's when I realized that I'd given her my bra size and not my age! I was fifty-seven, but I have great memories of my bra-size years!

I am making a serious effort to slow down after this morning. It was the final straw. It was a busy morning, and I remembered that I needed to make a dentist appointment.

I dug out my address book and found the number. I called my gynecologist and said, "I need to come in soon. I have a cavity that is growing and needs to be filled."

The receptionist could barely speak. She was laughing uncontrollably.

I didn't see the humor, so I told her, "This is serious. I could need a root canal!"

Now she was snorting in my ear. I was just ready to recommend a compounding shop for her hormones when she said, giggling, "Oh, Anne, you called the gynecologist, not the dentist."

Can you say 150 mental mph? My mind is like a NASCAR track.

My husband asked, "Why don't you just make a list and do one thing at a time, slowly?"

"I did that already. There are papers in the kitchen and the living room with my things-to-do-today. There might be a few in the family room, too."

"I meant on one single sheet of paper, in one place. Do it slowly," he counseled.

"Slowly? I'd never get anything done! The faster I go, the more I can accomplish in a day."

"Yes, like making a dentist appointment with your gynecologist? Telling the doctor you're as old as your chest?"

"I don't have time for this conversation. I'm getting behind on my schedule," I complained.

"There, do you see what I mean?" he moaned. "You are always in a rush!" He rolled his eyes and asked me to make him a drink.

"Can't do it right now," I told him. "I have to run to Wachovia Bank. I have to make a deposit."

"That's great," he said, "But our account is at Bank of America." Then he shook his head. "I'll make my own drink!"

Senioritis

t was January of 1998. My oldest daughter was about to graduate from high school in a few months. I called the guidance counselor and asked, "Have you put something in the drinking water?"

He laughed and said, "Oh, your child must be a senior!"

Erika, who was usually easygoing and pleasant, had developed a multiple personality disorder. One day, she was smiling and knew which colleges interested her. She was ready to travel, spread her wings, and live far from home. I felt proud, but I missed her already. I carried tissues in my pocket to mop my tears.

The very next morning, everything changed. Now she wanted to attend the college of her dreams. She had never visited this campus, but her friend told her there were hot guys there. It was two hours from home, just far enough that I couldn't visit too frequently. I bought a stress ball to carry along with the tissues in my pocket.

As the sun went down, things changed once more. She was not going to college now. Who needs hot boys anyway? She wanted to take some time to find herself. She'd find a job and live at home. She snarled as she reported this news. I felt queasy.

She stormed up the stairs and screamed, "It's my life, and I'll do what makes me happy! This decision makes me very happy." Then she slammed her door! She was NOT a poster child for happiness.

At this point, I carried a box of tissues strapped to my belt loop. If she leaves for college, I'd need them. If she really doesn't want me to visit, I'd need them. If she stays home, I'd need a bigger belt to carry the jumbo box around.

And so it went, day after day, week after week. I was living with three different personalities. Will someone please send my daughter back soon?

The teacher I'd spoken to was one of Erika's favorites. He assured me, "This is a difficult time for them. There's a lot of pressure to make big decisions, and they are all stressed."

My blood pressure rose. I wanted to jump through the phone. I almost screamed when I said, "Stressed? I'll show you stress. Live in our house with three of them, and then you'll know stress."

Now he was confused. "I didn't know you had triplets," he said.

"No, no, no! The three personalities and maybe a fourth ready to erupt," I said, trying to clarify. He now thought I was a crazy, stressed mother, which was totally true.

"This will all pass by June," he assured me.

"June? That's six months from now!" This was not good news.

This was worse than the terrible twos. Looking back, that was a breeze compared to the tornado under my roof now. It seemed as if it was just yesterday when she first learned the word, "No!" Right now, it was the most popular word in her vocabulary.

I just thought I could look forward to years with her living down the hall, music blaring, phone ringing all hours of the day and night. Now it dawned on me, that in a few months, she wouldn't be down our hall. She'd be in a dorm, down someone else's hall.

On one of our college visits, we were in a hotel room and she asked me to blow dry the back of her hair. As I brushed her hair, I looked in the mirror and staring back at me was my little three-year-old daughter.

The same face, same blue eyes, and the same smile. I wanted to jump through the mirror and go back in time. I wanted one more tea party, one more Johnjacobjingleheimerschmidt chorus in the car, and one more walk around the block with the baby dolls in her stroller. *Where did the years go?*

I decided that the best thing for me was to cherish those days and to love all three of my daughter's new personalities. I reminded myself that she was scared and under pressure and that I must enjoy my time with her today. I won't have this day again.

Tomorrow, I am buying stock in Kleenex!

ANNE BARDSLEY

Pretty Pretty

We were at a party one night when a male friend asked if we'd seen the billboard in Tampa.

"Which one?" I asked curiously.

He looked at his wife and grinned. "They haven't seen it. Can you tell?"

She giggled.

He went on, "There is a billboard advertising ... are you ready for this? Cosmetic Gynecology." As soon as he said the words, every woman in the room crossed their legs and began having contractions.

Thank God my mother is in heaven and she won't see this billboard. She called that entire region "Down Below." She always said it in a deep voice. To this day, when someone says, "Look down below," I shudder, even though they are talking about their kitchen cabinets.

Now I'm sure there are medical reasons for this surgery; I just don't like to imagine it. In fact, I'm afraid to check out my Down Below to see if I require such surgery.

Lately, I've been bombarded with commercials about my sagging eyes, double chin and, let's not forget, wrinkles (big and small). I just don't have the brain cells to add one more thing to my list of needed improvements.

I'm concerned that this billboard might cause minivans, Jaguars, and BMWs to drive right off the road and over the bridge.

Imagine you are a woman, driving along. You just lost your job, your kids are in trouble, and your husband is cheating. Then you come upon this billboard telling you that your Down Below is in need of beautification. *What do you do?*

The Department of Transportation should consider an exit ramp right there, so women can just drive right off into the Gulf of Mexico!

Seriously, what else could possibly need improvement on our bodies? To my knowledge, I don't believe that a single woman at that party thought they needed cosmetic surgery—Down Below.

How does this even come up in conversation?

"Mary, would you like white wine or red? I've been meaning to ask you, how is your vagina these days?"

"Oh, Jolene, thanks for asking. My husband thinks it needs cosmetic surgery."

Mary should immediately go over, whack Jolene's husband, and tell him to keep his eyes to himself! That's what a good girlfriend would do.

I remember when I asked my husband if I should get a facial rejuvenation. He put on his trifocal glasses, shrieked in horror, and reported that I have fur on my face. When I asked about my lines, he asked, "Do you want the big or small line count?" He also mentioned that my eyes looked droopy.

This did not go over well. I hid his glasses the very next day.

Imagine your boyfriend, husband, or both, mentioning that you might want to consider visiting the cosmetic gynecologist's office. I would get rid of them immediately. For the love of God, it's not as if we walk around on our hands!

I haven't seen a single billboard for men to have their Down Below touched up. Sure, they might want to make it bigger, but prettier? Less wrinkled? Men can take that blue pill and all is well in their underwear.

Why can't women have a pink touch-up pill? Even as I write the words, I wonder what I would touch up.

So ladies, I suggest that you just ignore that billboard. Even though you may have wrinkles, apparently they can be in other places, too, just stay vertical and smile. No one will ever know. We have larger issues to worry about.

We are so much more than just a pretty vagina!

The Clothes Bandit

We have a morning ritual in our house. At exactly 6:45 AM, I jump out of bed, brush my teeth, start the coffee, and feed the dogs.

I take my steaming hot coffee back to bed, prop myself, and wait for the show to begin.

At precisely 7:20 AM, my husband jumps in the shower, and at 7:30 AM every blessed morning, he tells me the exact same thing. It's like the movie *Groundhog Day*!

"My clothes are missing again," he says in the exact same tone he used the day before.

The daily saga goes like this: "I lost my favorite T-shirt, the one with the airplane on it. I saw it in the laundry room yesterday. Someone is stealing my clothes!"

I just smile and sip my coffee.

The next morning: "Someone stole my favorite running pants. Did you take them? The last time I saw them, they were in my drawer."

I just smile and sip my coffee.

Next morning: "Have you seen my workout clothes?

Someone took them out of the dryer. If you see anyone wearing my running pants, tackle them."

I just smile and sip my coffee.

There was a time when I'd jump up and run off in search of these missing, stolen clothes.

Then I switched to half-decaf coffee. Now I just smile. Every morning within the next ten minutes, he finds exactly what he had just sworn was stolen or hidden from him. It's usually in his drawers, although sometimes he hides things so that the people who are stealing his clothes won't find them.

Only problem is, he can't find them either.

Last week I found his gym clothes in the sunroom behind a big palm. I found his favorite low socks hidden behind the laundry soap in the garage. They are definitely in a good hiding place. No one would think to look there.

You'd think he'd stop announcing these lost items, *wouldn't you*? I mean, it's like admitting every morning that you are a moron, day after day.

Not that I'm perfect, mind you! Just this morning after he found his missing clothes, I announced once again, "My favorite bra is missing. We have a 'bra bandit' in our house."

"Well, it should be easy to spot him or her," he said. "They will be someone wearing my good low socks and your red bra. Let's call the police and ask if they can pick that person up." He chuckled.

I reminded him that my bra bandit was even more important than his clothes bandit. I'm too old to go free. This was serious!

He just sipped his coffee and smiled.

Quackers

Our kids have had pets of all different types over the years. It was the usual mix: cats, dogs, lizards, gerbils, and hermit crabs.

My favorite pets when I was growing up were the baby duck chicks that my dad brought home one Easter. We raised them until they were big enough to live on a farm. We named them Bonnie and Clyde.

They would follow my dad around as if he was their papa. They loved spaghetti. Their white chests were often smeared with spaghetti sauce and little pieces of noodles. They got a dunk in our pool after those meals. My mom was not so fond of the red spaghetti sauce skimming on top of the freshly cleaned pool.

Thirty years later, one fall day, a visitor arrived at our door. A brown, mallard duck decided to perch on our front porch. She was quite amusing. She'd quack like a watchdog when anyone came up the sidewalk. I fed her, because that's what moms do … we feed.

One day, Deufers, our cat, got too close to her. She flapped her wings at warp speed. She chased him down the driveway, waddling and squawking. Mr. Fearless ran off and climbed a nearby tree. Once he learned to keep his distance, they would sit side-by-side on the porch.

It was the funniest thing to watch. The cat and a duck sunning themselves, while we read the paper out front. I christened her, Quackers.

My son Michael is a hunter. The duck didn't seem to notice that. We have a picture of her sitting near his feet with the cat perched nearby. I guess she figured that if she could straighten out Deufers, she could handle Michael.

In just a few days, she became part of the family. We'd leave for work and leave her food and water. She'd be quacking and follow us to the car. We'd come home to her waddling down the sidewalk to greet us. I was falling in love with her.

Another week went by and a man knocked on our door. "I believe my daughter's duck has been visiting you," he said. "We've been looking for her. Jennifer will be so excited to see her."

I was not excited to see Quackers go.

He thanked us for taking such good care of her.

"I wonder why she chose your house," he said.

"I wondered too." I told him honestly. He scooped her up and took her home. I had tears in my eyes when they left. I missed her already.

My husband said, "Anne, you're getting all emotional about a duck!"

"Of course I am," I told him. He had no idea that I had cried all the way home from the farm when my dad dropped off Bonnie and Clyde.

The Note on the Door

have a very specific talent. I cannot juggle, do cartwheels, or win a baking contest. I can, however, write backward. I know you're wondering why I would even tell you this. Just try it. You'll see that it is not as easy as it may seem.

When our kids were small, the elves would leave notes. Every Christmas morning there were letters telling the kids how much they loved those cinnamon Snickerdoodles. The elves also wrote personal things that they'd seen happen over the year.

"Great goal last game!"

"That A+ on your spelling test was great!"

"We saw how nice you were to your sister!"

The elves wrote in the exact same penmanship as my backward cursive. *Who knew?*

On a more fun note, I once wrote my husband a note and left it on the front door where we had escaped to our little getaway vacation house. The note read, "We are so happy you and your wife are amorous, however, please close your windows. The children can hear you. My daughter asked whose dog was howling." I signed it, "A concerned neighbor."

I giggled as I taped it on the door. We were leaving to go to dinner when Scott spotted the note. "Anne, what is this?" he asked as he studied the note. "Oh no! The neighbors heard us!" He was horrified. Within ten seconds, he went from horrified to very proud of himself. I swear his chest swelled three inches.

We arrived at the restaurant and he asked, "Do you think this happens often?"

I said, "Often? Have we ever gotten a note before? No, it doesn't happen often!" It was all I could do not to burst out laughing.

"Which neighbor do you think left it? I'll be able to tell if the wife starts smiling at me."

"What are you talking about?"

He was getting ridiculously full of himself. "Well, you said it doesn't happen often. She probably thinks I'm a hottie."

Our shrimp cocktail arrived and the talk about the note continued. "She doesn't have very good handwriting," he said.

"She was probably nervous just bringing it over. Imagine if you had seen her at the door," I said, defending my penmanship.

"Well, when I get home I'm going to look out the bedroom window and try to figure this out. One of our neighbors knows we have sex now."

I finished my shrimp cocktail and hoped that this was the end of it.

After we finished dinner, he started up again, "So really, we do have a nice life, don't we?"

"Yes, we do," I said.

"Maybe the neighbor is envious of us."

"I don't think so," I told him as I rummaged in my purse for a pen.

I smiled to myself as I wrote on a napkin and passed it to him. There in my unique penmanship it read, "I wrote the note!"

"Are you serious? My God! You write like an elf!"

The Happy Dance

Our nest has been empty for a few years now and it is lovely. I never understood people who dreaded the day the house would be empty. Scott and I did the happy dance. It's a combination of the Mummers' Strut and Tina Turner wiggling her legs on stage. I heard that eagles put shards of glass in their nests to make it uncomfortable for the eaglets to stay in the nest. They are forced to take flight. We had done a good job and they were spreading their wings.

When we moved to Florida to semi-retire my husband set down a rule. We were going to have two knives, two forks, and two spoons. The plan included just enough for us. He refused to even buy a couch because he was convinced one of our five kids would try to sleep on it and root there. I was so proud that we were good eagle scouts, so to speak. It lasted less than six months.

Son number one came to visit and decided he should stay in Florida. He thought our guest room would be just perfect for him. Scott told him we only have two of everything. He went shopping and returned with plastic silverware and paper plates. He mentioned doing laundry and Scott announced that we have a very small washer and dryer. He should try the Laundromat.

My son looked back and forth from me to Scott and asked, "What? Why?"

"Yep, there's one right up the street," he told him. I thought this was a bit over the edge, but I left to do some itty bitty laundry in my teeny tiny washer. I let them work it out.

My son's phone rang and it was his brother telling him he might move down too. I overheard the conversation.

"You're going to need to bring knives, forks, spoons, paper plates, laundry detergent, and a lot of quarters. Oh, and a sleeping bag," he said as he scratched his head. "No, I'm serious. Dad is acting strange. You can't sleep on the couch or use his silverware. Oh, and the washer is very small. It's only big enough to do their wash."

I heard chatter on the other end of the phone, but all I could see was his facial expressions. He was staring at the ceiling repeating, "I know! I know! He's crazy! I'm serious."

"You better call and tell them you're thinking of moving here. I'm not telling them. Maybe we should look for an apartment."

The happy dance continued!

The Twelve Days of Hormones

I went to my doctor to get my hormone levels tested. Don't you know, my progesterone is very low. I'm convinced that this is the hormone responsible for working out, keeping the house tidy, and creating delicious gourmet meals. I think it may even have some control over sexual desire. I should've known something wasn't right. I was just feeling horizontal lately—as in, I lay down at every opportunity, hence, no gym, no vacuuming, no exotic dinners … no thoughts of wild times under the sheets.

In addition to my progesterone, my testosterone is also a tad low. My doctor said I needed hormone replacement therapy, but he warned that I may grow hair, my voice may get deeper, and my libido may increase with my new hormone routine. I'm hoping I don't start scratching my groin in public, too.

"So you're telling me that I may get hairy, have a deep voice, and feel amorous?" I laughed. "That is my husband's worst nightmare." I laughed harder.

We have been married thirty-five years, and we are really pretty good together. We can talk about anything and everything. There are no secrets. Until now. Do I really want to tell him what could happen to me once the hormones kick in? Maybe he won't notice. No need to scare the poor man away.

I began the hormone replacement therapy.

On the first day of hormones, no change.

On the second day of hormones, I felt a bit amorous.

On the third day of hormones, I noticed more hair on my armpits.

On the fourth day, I looked at myself in the mirror, and I heard myself say, "Looking good, Baby!" in a husky voice. This cannot be happening.

On the fifth day of hormones, I felt the need to tug at my crotch.

On the sixth day, Scott said, "Your voice is getting deeper than mine."

On the seventh day of hormones, I bought a set of barbells.

On the eighth day, Scott asked, "Is that a mustache on your face?"

On the ninth day of hormones, I told Scott he was acting like a girl.

On the tenth day, he asked, "Were you staring at me in the shower this morning?"

On the eleventh day, Scott woke up with a sunburn. Apparently, I had a hot flash that night.

On the twelfth day, we were at a nice restaurant and I asked, "Want to arm wrestle?"

I knew my testosterone was in high gear when I heard myself ask, "Can you teach me to field strip an M-16 and put it back together blindfolded? I really want to go to the shooting range."

His response was short and sweet. "I want that doctor's number and I want it now!"

The Ugly Baby

When my oldest daughter, Erika, was eight months pregnant, her hormones rocked and rolled. She called one day in tears.

"Mom, what if I have an ugly baby and no one tells me she's ugly?" she sobbed into the phone. "Who would have the heart to tell a mom that her baby is ugly? I'll go through life thinking I have a beautiful baby and everyone else will know she's ugly."

I suppressed a chuckle. "You're going to have a beautiful baby. Don't even let the universe hear you say those words. Yell 'Cancel!'"

"Cancel," she said quietly. "Mom, will you promise to tell me if the baby is ugly?" she sniffled.

"Of course! I'll be totally honest," I promised, thinking this would calm her.

She screeched, "No, you won't! You already think she's beautiful, and you haven't even seen her." I had to agree. Maybe someone else would tell us both.

When she mentioned this worry to her husband Brett, his response was pure shock. "Hello! Have you looked at me lately?"

He struck a model pose. "There is no way we could have an ugly baby." This made her stop crying until another wave of hormones rolled in.

My husband offered to be the ugly baby judge. The problem is he thinks all newborns are ugly. He likes them at six months. "Scott, you can't be the judge! You don't like babies and their wrinkled little faces. If you tell her she has an ugly baby, it will crush her."

I reminded him of the time we visited the nursery and all he could say was, "They shouldn't show these babies yet. Look at them! One is uglier than the next."

I had to shoo him down the hall fast. Proud parents were arriving to bask in the glow of their newborns. I could hear the oohing and aahing as I pushed Scott down the corridor.

The day finally arrived in August. Kaylee had ten perfect fingers and ten perfect toes. She had no wrinkles on her little round face. Her eyes were open, and I swear she smiled at me when I first held her.

The only thing I could compare that feeling to is holding a miracle, a priceless miracle. I passed her papoose-wrapped body to her new pop, and we waited. She snuggled into his arms. I think I saw a tear in his eye.

"Now this is the most beautiful baby I have ever seen!" he proclaimed.

The judge had spoken! The Ugly Baby Case was closed!

I've since had two more grandbabies. The judge has been called back to court twice and again ... a beautiful baby verdict was declared.

The Punk on the Beach

My mother-in-law once told me, "Anne, you and Scott laugh too much for a married couple." Then she frowned at me. I got the message. Pipe down with the happiness!

We've raised five kids, owned a business, and we've had our share of stress. We just choose to live life on the lighter side.

About six months ago, Scott became a Eucharistic minister. He serves Communion every Sunday at church. He feels very blessed and honored to do this. He looks like a big altar boy as he floats down the aisle in his white robe.

When he passes me, he gives me a smile and a wink. I wink back and give him a smooch face. I love this man!

One Sunday after church, we went to the beach for some sun. Our daughter, Jamie, was visiting, after just finishing grad school. As we stood in line to order lunch at the beach café, a young woman wearing a New Jersey T-shirt got in line behind us.

Scott mentioned that he spent every summer at the Jersey shore as a kid, and she gave him all the latest news.

After we sat in our chairs on the beach, who should arrive but Miss Jersey.

"Hey! Jersey guy, I need your help."

"What kind of help?" Scott asked.

"We're playing a game. Come on. It'll be fun," she said.

Off he went six beach towels over. Within a few minutes, we heard laughter coming from that area, so I decided to investigate.

As I approached, I noticed they had set up an impromptu beauty pageant. It looked like the swimsuit competition for Miss America.

There were four judges in beach chairs. Sand castles bordered the runway, which passed through the judging area. Scott was judge number two.

Each judge had large cards numbered in black—eight through ten. They also had "Fake" and "Real" signs to complete their scorecards.

The judges attracted the attention of women walking on the beach. There were many participants, all in good fun. The neighboring sunbathers were clapping, which inspired the contestants.

The women were now dancing. Contestant number one was showing off her gymnastic ability. Contestant number two posed like a model in a photo shoot with the wind blowing through her hair. She pouted her lips in hopes that the honorable judges would raise her score. Angelina Jolie would have been proud.

I headed back to my chair.

"So what's happening over there?" Jamie asked. "Do I want to know?"

"Your father is a judge, and he has cards with eight, nine, and ten on them. He also has signs saying Real and Fake."

She leaned back in her chair and peeked over her sunglasses.

"Are you serious? Tell me you're kidding!"

Just then, a middle-aged woman wandered over and asked, "What did they want your husband to do?"

I explained and she laughed. We introduced ourselves. Marilyn was on vacation from New York. I leaned in a little closer and asked her to do me a favor. "Can you just go over there and ask him if he gave you Communion this morning?" She grinned and said, "Anne, I like your style!"

Jamie and I watched Marilyn saunter over to the catwalk. She was swaying her hips and flipping her hair. She had the judges' attention! They gave her two eights, two nines, and a Real sign. She got closer to Scott, tapped him on the shoulder, and asked, "Aren't you a Eucharist minister? I think you gave me Communion this morning. Should you be doing this?"

He sat straight up and did his best Linda Blair impersonation from the movie *The Exorcist*. His head spun to the far left, then right. He was scanning the area for fellow Catholics who received Communion that morning.

Just then, Jersey girl said, "Scott, you are so busted!"

He scampered back to our beach chairs, wearing sunglasses and a floppy army hat. He was incognito! "Oh, my God! You are not going to believe this," he told us. "Someone recognized me from church. I gave her Communion this morning! Oh, this is so not good." He sank back into his chair.

"Dad, she recognized you?" Jamie asked, "Are you sure you gave her Communion?"

His voice was shaky as he responded, "Yes, I'm sure! Can you believe it?"

We both responded at the same time. "No! What are the chances of that happening?"

To make things even better, Marilyn stopped by to chat.

Scott asked her, "How did you recognize me?" He was still baffled that this could happen.

She deserved an Academy Award, when she replied, "Oh, it was easy. I recognized your mustache and those broad shoulders."

He forgot that he was in potential hot water and started puffing out his chest. He moved his shoulders to show her what he's got.

"By the way, you looked like a football player when you came down the aisle in that robe."

At this point, I don't think he knew if he should say "thank you" or run home.

About that time, our friend Tracey arrived at the beach. I immediately mouthed the words, "Just go along with this." She grinned back at me.

Scott immediately confessed to her.

She looked appropriately shocked. "Scott, what were you thinking? Eucharistic ministers can't behave like that."

Jamie was now smirking in her towel. I just sat with a bewildered look on my face. "Jamie, pass the suntan lotion, please. I don't want to be as red as your father when he burns in hell for his actions." The three of us cracked up. Scott saw no humor in this conversation whatsoever.

The next morning, Scott moaned that he had a terrible dream. "The church called me in and fired me." I immediately put a pillow over my head and pretended to have a coughing fit.

He was so upset with his behavior that he started telling everyone what he did. He told people at work. He called family and friends. He even called my eighty-five-year-old Catholic Aunt Helen to ask for ideas for penance. He also mentioned to her that he gave everyone a nine score and they all got Real signs.

My aunt said, "Well, Scott, I'm not sure that's going to be enough to get you into Heaven."

The next Sunday, Scott sat in his robe, reading his prayer book before Mass started. He opened to a page that told about the behavior of a Eucharistic minister and read, "You must always carry yourself in a responsible manner and never act in a way that would embarrass the church." He snapped the book shut and closed his eyes. He was convinced God was sending him a message.

The next day, as he was preparing to leave town on business, he said, "I hope that woman isn't on the plane."

I realized that this was torturing him. It wasn't funny anymore. I had to tell him. "You didn't give her Communion," I confessed.

He stared and me and said, "Yes I did! She recognized me."

I felt very guilty. "I punked you," I confessed. "I asked her to tell you that you had given her Communion. I have no idea who that woman was. She was just a random stranger on the beach, playing along. She won't be on the plane."

"No, Marilyn recognized me. Stop trying to make me feel better. I'm going to call the church and ask if there have been any reports about my behavior so I can tell my side of the story."

Now I was beginning to sweat. "You can't call the church and report this. They'll fire you! Seriously, I punked you."

He stepped back and started to laugh. "Are you serious? You punked me? Jamie knew? Tracey knew? You really got me!" he laughed, looking relieved. "That was great!" He laughed all the way to the car, saying, "I've been punked!"

I'm a little nervous now. You know what they say about paybacks.

September Blues

I always hated September. When our house was full with five kids, it meant a lot of running around and preparation, gathering back-to-school supplies. I would usually be scampering around at the last minute, looking for black-and-white marbled copybooks.

Each store would have two or three, and we needed twenty-five.

Now, I know this was partly my fault for procrastinating, but the last thing I wanted to hear from each and every store clerk was, "Didn't this happen last year, too?" The older woman at the drug store actually smirked.

"No! I have a twin sister!" I stormed out the door. It happened again at the discount department store. The clerk remembered that I had been very frazzled this time last year as well.

Seriously, where do these people get their memories? I could barely remember to pick up twenty-five copybooks, let alone recognize cashiers from last year.

When I mentioned this to the store clerk, she laughed and said, "Oh, you've been frazzled every year for the past five years!" It seems that I had a reputation.

In addition to the twenty-five copybooks, there was a three-page list of supplies for each child, each one different in some way.

There were also eighty-five forms to fill out, in case one of them got a fever at school.

Then there was a two-page memo regarding appropriate attire for class. They wore uniforms! How much more info did we need?

Apparently, the knee socks could be only one shade of blue, and laces had to be tied on the approved style of dock siders. There was a drawing showing the acceptable length of the skirt. It was exactly in the middle of the kneecap.

The boys had to wear navy or khaki pleated pants with golf shirts, which were only sold by the uniform company. I could find these shirts in other stores for $12.99, but we had to buy the $24.99 brand from the uniform company. Don't even ask!

All that was nothing compared to the problems with backpacks. We needed five different colors. The last thing I needed on a Monday morning was to get a call from the school, saying that Erika had Mike's backpack.

They went to two different schools, and something like that meant pure aggravation for one unhappy mom who had to drive all over town to switch the bags. I actually got to the point where, if they called to say they had forgotten their lunch, I told them to beg for food from a friend. They stopped forgetting their lunches by the third week of school.

Then, there was the activity schedule! I would get up on a beautiful fall Saturday morning, with the plan to plant mums. However, my plans changed immediately. The kids had places to go and people to see.

8:00— sip coffee, preparing for my day in the garden

8:30— cancel nice morning and gulp more coffee

9:00— take Erika to tennis practice

9:30— take Michael to football practice

10:00— take Jamie to gymnastics

11:00— pick up Erika from tennis and rush to football field for Michael

11:30— drop Erika off at volleyball practice

11:45— pick Jamie up from gymnastics

12:00— drive Justin to hockey practice

12:15— drop Michael off to buy lizard food

12:30— open bag of pretzels for lunch and snooze in car while he shops for lizard food

1:00— go back to pick Erika up from volleyball

1:30— drop Tom at his friend's house

2:00— go back to hockey to pick up Justin

2:30— go grocery shopping

3:00— pick up Jamie's friend and take her to our house

3:30— stop for ice cream to delay hunger pangs

3:35— find out that Erika forgot her jacket at volleyball, drive over to fetch it

3:45— realize I forgot to get dinner while grocery shopping

4:00— go back to grocery store and stop to get wine

4:30— pick up Tom at his friend's house

5:00— Scott comes home and says, "You were lucky! You had the day off!"

5:05— pass out on the couch!

Mothers-in-law

When people ask if I get along with my mother-in-law, I can honestly say, yes. Especially now that she is in Heaven. She was a bit of a pip.

She was very outspoken and gave her opinion, whether you wanted it or not. So when people ask how Scott became so easy going, I tell them the truth. I say with a straight face, "He was hatched!"

Her real name was Anna Dorothy, but her nickname was Dodi. When our kids were little, she asked that they call her Dodi instead of Grandmom. And so they did.

There were times in my life when I wondered if my husband was really a prince, because his mom had a tendency to believe she was, indeed, a queen.

The first time I met Dodi was at the New Jersey shore. She'd made a great dinner. All was well until she served dessert. She placed a martini glass filled with fresh strawberries in front of each of us.

That's when it happened. I merely plucked one of the strawberries off the top of my glass and popped it into my mouth. I heard her gasp. I hadn't noticed the child-sized spoon on my martini's glass plate.

No one said anything about it then. But the next day, Scott said, "Did you see my mother's face when you ate that strawberry with your fingers?"

I crunched my brows and darted my eyes from side-to-side while in a panic. I wondered why that was a problem.

"She was horrified that you didn't use the spoon."

"That spoon was so small it looked like it belonged in a dollhouse! I would have spilled the berries all over myself! Who has silverware like that, anyway?" I snarled.

"Uh ... my mother," he replied with a grin.

Years later, we bought brand new family room furniture. We replaced a yard-sale black, white, and tan floral sectional.

Depending where you sat on that old sofa, a spring could shake loose and goose you in the butt. We thought the new furniture was just beautiful. We both felt so proud that we'd saved the money to buy it.

We invited my in-laws over, and when Dodi walked into the family room, she just sat on the couch. She never said a word about the new furniture. So my husband asked, "Is the sofa comfortable?" leading her into a compliment.

"Yes, it's fine," Dodi replied. Then she sneezed and remarked that she must be allergic to the dust in our house. She obviously believed she was a queen. I believe the English call this "damning with faint praise."

Over the years, I became accustomed to Dodi's ways. The final straw happened a few months before she died.

Scott received a phone call that his parents needed help up north; both were in poor health. So as a good son, he left Florida to go and help out.

Dodi was receiving dialysis treatments three times a week. On one visit, he drove to pick her up and waited in the lobby. He heard his mother telling the nurse to check to see if her son was there yet.

She described him as, "The short, fat, bald guy." (I don't think queens talk like that, do they?)

It became a family joke. Our nieces would call up and ask, "Can I speak to SFBG, please?"

My brother-in law called to ask, "I need help moving next week. Is the SFBG available to help?"

One day, Scott asked, "Mom, seriously? A short, fat, bald guy? Is that the best you can say?"

She replied, "Well, I guess you're not all that short, and you really are a prince of a son." That was the nicest thing a queen could say.

Summer Vacation at the Beach

ast week, Scott and I sat watching a young family frolic on the beach. Two of the young kids, covered in sand from nose to toes, were diligently creating a sandcastle.

The dad was splashing in the water with the older child. The young mom was preparing picnic food for her entire family from her gingham-lined basket. When lunch was ready, they all gathered on the blanket and enjoyed Mom's homemade sandwiches. It was like a Norman Rockwell picture.

My "bad memory alert" button started flashing in my head as I remembered our summer vacations with five kids. They ranged in age from one to nine. My in-laws owned a home at the Jersey shore, so we'd stay there for our long-awaited getaway vacation.

Our days would start out with a fight over breakfast. Then there would be an argument over who would go in the bathroom first. Next, there would be a battle over who took the other's juice. It just kept getting better and better. After thirty minutes of this, I locked myself in the bathroom.

Then I heard my husband take charge. "Tom, you are in charge of getting the Frisbee and football. Mike, you get the fishing rods and bait. Erika, put the toy buckets and shovels into the red wagon. Jamie, pack up the baby dolls. Justin, get your red truck."

In addition to two wagons, we carried beach umbrellas, the baby's walker, a small high chair, and a playpen to the beach. We also toted a huge cooler filled with sandwiches, juice boxes, and snacks. By the time we unloaded the Suburban at the boardwalk, I was miserable. I wanted to go back, re-lock myself into the bathroom, and just cry.

After four trips across the hot sand, we had our beach quilt spread out and our campsite set up. Within three minutes, sand covered everything. Little feet were walking in every possible direction. Justin, the one-year-old, was innocent. I only know this because he refused to walk in the sand. Once we relocated him to the sandy blanket, he refused to leave.

Next, Scott had to hoist the umbrella from the wagon and pound it into the sand to shade our pale bodies from the sun. This took fifteen minutes and a lot of bad language on my husband's part. We all clapped for him when it was in place.

Next was setting up the playpen. "DO NOT let sand get in the playpen," I warned, as the rails snapped into place. The baby walker was a wasted effort to bring along because Justin just lifted his legs like a frog to avoid touching the sand and screamed.

Wow! Time goes fast when you go to the beach. We no sooner got our "beach camp" set up and it was lunchtime. By now, my hair was blowing in my sweaty face. I should've made sandwiches the way Scott had suggested, but I thought it would be nice to let each kid place an order (I must have seen a Rockwell beach picnic painting somewhere!).

I'd forgotten all of the condiments ... no mayo, no butter, no mustard. This did not go over well. I told the kids that fish could smell mayo and mustard on their breath, and they'd never catch a fish that way.

Somewhere between complaints of sand in their bread and spilled juice, I nodded off. I think it was a combination of the coffee wearing off and me having heat stroke, to be perfectly honest.

We'd been at our beach encampment for approximately thirty minutes when I heard a loud buzzing noise. I thought, "Oh no!" A herd of green flies attacked my legs. No one else's, just mine. It was as if they were having a smorgasbord on my poor, pale legs. I screamed, swatted, and ran into the water, hoping to drown the big buggers.

A surfer's wave toppled me from the rear. I hate salt water. It turns my blonde hair green. The damn flies were swirling around my head. They were like piranhas with wings and I was their next meal. I swatted and cursed at them. I staggered toward the beach as another wave toppled me into the water. My hair was plastered on my face. I lost my new sunglasses. My bathing suit top slipped and exposed my left breast. I was choking up disgusting sea water and my language was not very lady-like, much less mother-like.

My husband and the kids found this extremely funny. They rolled in the sand, laughing. I was furious! If I were a better swimmer, I would have swum out to sea and hitched a ride on a fishing boat.

Just as I collapsed on the beach blanket, my husband said, "Oh, I forgot to tell you. My mother called and she's coming down to spend the rest of the week with us.

I went back in the water to play with the green flies.

My Favorite Gift That I'll Never Receive

I haven't received my favorite gift yet, but I've seen it. And I love it! This gift has become even more special, coveted even, in the past few days. My oldest daughter, Erika, bought me a small, scalloped picture frame as a Mother's Day gift. The edges are scalloped and it's red. I'm thinking my granddaughter, Kaylee, may have chosen the color. She likes bright colors and so do I.

Erika chose a photo of the day her younger daughter, Riley, was born. I'm holding Riley in her snuggly blanket and Kaylee is looking down at her new sister. It is a very sweet memory for me. Riley was just a few hours old with her chubby little cheeks and lips pursed. Kaylee was mesmerized every time she moved.

"It's my baby sister, baby Riley," she'd say over and over. She still calls her Baby Riley. I have the feeling Riley will be going off to college and Kaylee will say, "Have fun at college, Baby Riley."

When Erika got the wrapping paper ready, the photo disappeared. It seems Kaylee decided she should keep this gift. She stuffed it in her white purse with multi-color hearts. She brings it everywhere. She even ripped the stand off the back so it would fit better in that purse of hers.

Erika called to tell me, "Mom, my daughter is a thief!"

At night, she places the picture on her night stand, along with a picture she keeps of Pop and her at the pool. He is standing in the water and she's perched on the pool deck with her legs dangling. They are deep in conversation in one of those discussions that goes like this:

"Come on, Kaylee! Jump in and I'll catch you."

"Wait, Pop, I see an ant. I need to follow him first. Stay right here and I'll be back."

"No! Come on. It's fun in the water."

"I know, Pop, but the ant might be lost."

She makes sure the ant makes it to the grassy area.

She returns a minute later, confident that the ant is safe.

"Okay, Pop, here I come! Catch me!" she shouts, as she hurls herself toward him.

We have a place of honor in her little world. She holds us, not only in her purse, but in her heart. You couldn't give me a bag of gold to replace these moments.

This is definitely my favorite gift that I'll never receive. And that's just fine with me.

www.ingramcontent.com/pod-product-compliance
Lightning Source LLC
Chambersburg PA
CBHW070959040426
42443CB00007B/580